Decorative Art
and Modern Interiors

Decorative Art
and Modern Interiors 1978

Studio Vista
London

Van Nostrand Reinhold Company
New York Cincinnati Toronto London Melbourne

volume 67 edited by Maria Schofield

Cover
The guest room in the converted
loft of 'The Home of the Architect
in Aalst, Belgium'
architect: Pieter de Bruyne
photography: Gé Meijnen fotograaf

Title page
Interplay of light and reflections:
the South West elevation of 'The
Hilton Hotel in Budapest, Hungary'
architect: Béla Pintér
photography: István Vidovics

A Studio Vista book publication by
Cassell & Co, Ltd,
35 Red Lion Square, London WC1 4SG
and at Sydney, Auckland, Johannesburg
an affiliate of
Macmillan Publishing Co Inc
New York

Copyright © Studio Vista 1978
First published in 1978

Published in 1978 by
Van Nostrand Reinhold Company
A division of Litton Educational Publishing, Inc
450 West 33rd Street, New York, NY 10001, USA

Van Nostrand Reinhold Limited
1410 Birchmount Road
Scarborough, Ontario M1P 2E7, Canada

Library of Congress Catalog Card Number 76-29529
U.S. ISBN 0-442-27421-1
U.K. ISBN 0-289-707-84-6

Designed by Marie-Louise Luxemburg
Set in Monophoto Optima 10 on 11 pt by
Tradespools Ltd, Frome, Somerset, England
Separations by Colorlito, Milano, Italy
Printed and bound in Italy by SAGDOS Spa, Milano
16 15 14 13 12 11 10 9 8 7 6 5 4 3 2 1

Contents

Acknowledgements

The Editor wishes to thank all architects, designers and manufacturers who supplied illustrations for reproduction

Introduction

Today we associate technology with machines; but in societies of old that honoured the work of hand and tool, technology was closely allied to manual skills. Series production of a model was often practised during the Renaissance; and later, in the 17th century, multiples were sometimes used in workshops as a matter of expedience. A classical example exists, by two disciples of the sculptor Giambologna, Pietro Tacca and Antonio Susini, who used to produce multiples of interchangeable parts of equestrian monuments: horses, bodies, heads, that could be assembled without having to create original work each time. Yet, this still involved individual choice: a choice made, for the need of a particular society, by members of that society. In consequence, the work itself became part of the common heritage. This combination of individual requirements and technology is recognizable in the shape of old buildings, and determined the planning of cities. When observing a medieval village in remote parts of central Italy, we are intrigued by how the irregular roofline of the houses, climbing row upon row towards the main piazza, possesses a rigorous rhythm of its own, an authority of expression born of the very slow, painstaking process of building those houses made to last for generations.

It is perhaps because of this that a sense of permanence lingers on old places, enhanced rather than diminished by the ravages of time and the destructions of war, inspiring us to restore and put to new use buildings from the past; and also, to keep alive old traditional skills or to search in museums and bookshops for records of lost ones. It seemed apt, then, to include in this 67th edition of 'Decorative Art' examples of work that express a wish to return to a tradition that we all share. This in itself is not new; but it acquires a new emphasis because such tradition is under attack by a modern world marked by transience and mechanization.

In his *Hamar Museum near Oslo*, Sverre Fehn encloses the remains of a medieval barn within a modern building, leaving the ruins untouched. Béla Pintér incorporates remains from many ages in his *Hilton Hotel in Budapest*, an amazing exercise in architectural restraint, both sensitive and vigorous. Other examples, though less impressive in scale, demonstrate different ways of reacting to the traditions of the past. *The Home of the Architect in Aalst, Belgium*, by Pieter de Bruyne, expresses a metaphysical concept of space through ingenious planning and a highly individual use of common materials. *An Apartment in Palazzo Erizzo*, by Aureliano Pastor, is a design solution to the contrast between contemporary life-style and architectural conservation of a 17th century Venetian palace. In the United States and in England, examples of imaginative extensions and conversions are given by the firm of Helmuth Obata & Kassabaum and George Ranalli; and by John Guest, Steven Le Roith and Alan Coles, in London, Keith Garbett in Cambridge; while in France, *The Country House of the Architect near Paris*, by Alain Richard, retains in the well-appointed modern interior the rugged, wholesome character of the traditional stone house.

A similar approach has directed the choice of this year's special feature. The revival of interest in early music performance during the last decade, and its inevitable influence on the music trade, resulted in a keen demand for restoration and reproduction of old musical instruments. Today, reproductions of ancient tribal percussion instruments are sought for use in schools, and specialist publications gain a steadily increasing readership. A trade fair organized in London by the Early Music Shop, in September 1977, ended with a successful auction sale led by Sotheby's, the first, on that firm's records, to be devoted primarily to early music instruments. Among the items offered there were twenty-two violins and violas of the 18th and early 19th century, in original condition – a very rare find, since the great majority of stringed instruments was modified, at the beginning of the past century, to withstand the increased tension on the sound-board due to the standardization of sound pitch. These instruments, though not of exceptional quality, were sought by dealers, collectors and professional musicians not just for their historical value but because the whole business of early music-making today is based on the study of antique instruments. Never before in musical history has the commitment to the past been so absolute. In many cases the maker is so absorbed in the process of re-creation that he surrenders his own individuality to the point of reproducing the original ornamentation; on other occasions there is an emphasis on old construction techniques; this has in turn led to researching and reproducing special tools that had become collectors' items, and to re-learning their use so that the final piece could be a faithful replica of the original in every respect. There is also, of course, the tendency to take advantage of modern resources and materials, as for example the use of plywood, or of delrin, for certain parts of plucked string or keyboard instruments. In her article 'Instruments for Early Music by Today's Makers', Fiona Adamczewski outlines the background history of this revival and its recent developments both in Europe and the United States.

In furniture-making, two interesting factors are noticeable: firstly, an encouraging number of young English craftsmen have established their own independent workshops; secondly, Scandinavian design, drawing fresh impetus from technological progress, is now taking the lead from Italy.

The work of John Makepeace could well be the force behind the English furniture revival. In an attempt to overcome the problem of the inadequate facilities available to young craftsmen, John Makepeace opened his workshops to talented people willing to accept the strict discipline of his method of work. Established craftsmen in their own right such as David Field, Ashley Cartwright, Bill Hall, were among his first apprentices. In Spring 1977 John Makepeace took over Parnham House, a 16th century mansion surrounded by gardens and parkland in the Dorset countryside. The house, extended by John Nash in the 18th century, was carefully adapted to become *The John Makepeace School for Craftsmen in Wood*. Students are offered a residential, intensive two-year training, not just in furniture-making but also in the practical activities of running an office, marketing, general management, and setting up a workshop. During their stay at the school, students are expected to identify a potential market for their work, in order to rely on their own resources. Ten students, aged from 18 to 26, were accepted in the School's first year of activity. Their varied educational backgrounds include Law, Engineering and Languages, and range from University entry to post-graduate levels. To our knowledge this is the first, and so far the only organization in Europe offering training for self-employment.

In the furniture industry there is a marked return to natural materials; the varied, subtle textures of wood are replacing the gloss of plastics. Possibly two economic factors account for the swing of the pendulum: plastics are no longer cheap and wood is plentiful, at least in Scandinavia. However, in the opinion of Christian Hellesøe, Managing Director of Johannes Hansen AS, this change would have come about in any case; there has been too much indiscriminate use of plastics in the past, and plastics do not age gracefully. By tradition, good Scandinavian industrial design rests upon three main foundations: style, function, and feeling for materials; the best Danish furniture, as exhibited at the Bella Centre and at Den Permanente in Copenhagen, shows a clear evidence of the old cabinet-making tradition in rural Denmark. The strength deriving from this is recognized by the Scandinavian furniture industry, and every effort is made to maintain a link with tradition; for example, every craftsman it employs has served a minimum four years' apprenticeship in workshops, and furniture designers are expected to make their own prototypes. 'In every production line of a model there is a fall in quality', affirms Hans Wegner, who himself served an apprenticeship as a cabinet-maker; therefore, the designer never loses touch with production, and two expert supervisors are responsible for machine and for hand-finishing work. In consequence, every piece reveals the extent of the involvement of a team of dedicated specialists. These pieces could well become part of a wider common heritage, eventually find their place in museums as well as in homes, to benefit a richer cultural life of a larger, more discerning society.

Maria Schofield

Architectural Conservation and Modern Living

The Hilton Hotel in Budapest, Hungary

architect:
Béla Pintér
Közti Architectural and
Engineering Office for
Public Buildings

photography:
István Vidovics

The city of Budapest spreads over a relatively wide area, yet contains, with just over 2,000,000 inhabitants, about 20% of the entire population of Hungary. It is therefore one of the very few modern capital cities still free from the pressures of urban development, able to retain the architectural image of a great historical past. This privilege calls, however, for a particular expertise when planning an entirely new building, as was indeed the case with the Hilton Hotel. One is immediately aware of the irksome difficulties facing the architect by just looking at the plan of the building. The site, the historical centre of the city of Buda, is on a steep hill overlooking the Danube and the city of Pest over the plain beyond. The hill is surrounded by the recon-structed medieval ramparts of the Fishermen's Bastion. The Gothic Matthias Church is there, and also some very attractive 17th century buildings such as the first public hotel in the Castle District, 'At the Sign of the Red Porcupine', now being converted into a res-taurant. The intended location of the hotel was, therefore, the focal centre of the capital in every respect.

The actual area to be covered included a medieval street, some old cellars, remains of a medieval tower, a 13th century Dominican church with its cloister, and the facade of a 18th century Jesuit college and chapel. All this had to be preserved at all cost. The archi-tectural solution was eventually a purely

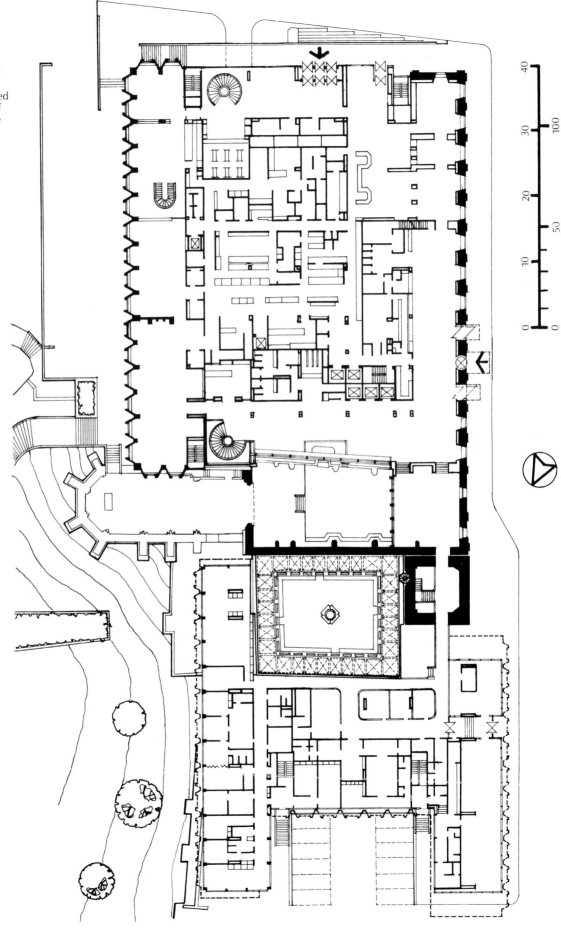

2 Outside view showing, as if
in a collage, the remains of
buildings from past ages linked
by the continuing roof line of
the new hotel block, left. The
turret on the Gothic tower is
contemporary

3 Ground floor plan

4 The entrance hall, from the reception desk; at the far end, left, can be seen one of the Roman milestones that marked the boundary of the Roman Empire along the Danube; the stone was found during excavations on site

5 The main lobby, seen from the first floor

6 One of the 323 bedrooms, comfortably equipped with individually controlled air conditioning, direct-dial telephone, radio, private bath

Overpage
7 The restored nave of a 13th century church, and the new hotel elevation opposite, define an open area that has excellent acoustic properties. In the Summer of 1977, the year the hotel was opened, a series of concerts devoted to Medieval and Renaissance music was held there. See illustration 9, opposite, taken during a rehearsal

modular one: a design grid based on a 3.75m square related both to the existing elements and to the space requirements of a modern luxury hotel.

The structure is reinforced concrete, column and slab construction in the public spaces and crosswall construction in the bedroom areas. The building is clad in reinforced concrete sandwich panels, designed to give a high level of thermal insulation. To balance the heaviness of the concrete facade, bronze-coloured glass is used to great advantage, especially in the part facing North-East.

The appearance of the main facade could aptly be described as an architectural collage.

Looking at the fish-eye view on page 2 we can see, left, the new wing linked by a brief passage to the medieval tower; adjoining the tower is the reconstructed facade of the Jesuit college; to the extreme right of the spire of Matthias Church can just be seen. The severe roofline of the new building, briefly interrupted by the tower, brings into evidence the elegant proportions of the Baroque facade, and at the same time gives it the illusion of being two-dimensional, like a stage backdrop.

The unobtrusive entrance to the hotel leads into an L-shaped reception and lobby area. Full height glazed panels give light to the main lobby and separate the monumental part of the building from the strictly functional block.

9 An orchestra rehearsing for
an open air concert in the
former nave of the 13th century
Dominican Church

10 One of the restaurants, named after the Kalocsa region famous for the characteristic patterns of its folk art. Traditional Hungarian dishes are served here

At the far end of the lobby a spiral staircase leads to a lower level foyer and thence to an open space, once the nave of the Gothic church. This is undoubtedly the most significant of the existing ruins, to which the whole architectural concept is closely related. For it is to the existence of the only surviving North-West wall of this church that we owe Béla Pintér's idea of separating the total building into two blocks, one in harmony with the formal Baroque facade, the other of more irregular shape, yet governed by the discipline of the germinal module, repeated in rhythmic sequence throughout. The dramatic impact is indeed powerful: a truncated wall, ochre-coloured, seems to cut like a blade through the two massive blocks of concrete and glass.

The treatment of the interior spaces shows lack of continuity with the basic architecture – a condition to be sadly regretted whenever the architect does not design the whole building, and distinctions between 'architecture' and 'interior decoration' are allowed to destroy the unity of his concept. With the exception of the circulation areas and of the bedrooms, where the design is reasonably restrained and directed to provide maximum comfort, there is too much concern about reproducing the atmosphere of bygone ages without the ability to express it in the idiom of our time; and this ability seems to be the supreme achievement of Béla Pintér.

11, 12 Two views of the Coffee Shop, where breakfast and light meals are served. Dark oak panelling and furniture evoke the cool atmosphere of a traditional farmhouse

9

13 An example of architectural conservation in the passage to the Dominican cloister

14 The ambulatorium of the former 13th century cloister has been renovated on the basis of the original architecture; archaeological remains on stone plinths, and photographs of the old city along the walls add to the peaceful atmosphere of this space; in the background can be seen the distant dome of the House of Parliament

Opposite
15 Another view of the cloister, with contemporary additions, and of the restored original stone well

Overpage
16 The North-East elevation, from the ramparts of the Fishermen's Bastion. In the centre foreground are the ruins of the church nave, with the new turret of the Gothic tower beyond

The Caravelle Celine Boutique in Milan, Italy

architect:
Sergio Asti

photography:
Giorgio Casali

This boutique, in an area of Milan famous for its elegance and for many ancient buildings, occupies an irregular, deep, narrow space on three levels, opening onto a busy piazza near the Cathedral. Therefore, the architect's idea was to create an arresting, exciting design that would not be loud or pretentious.

The entire facade is glass, so that the whole interior can be seen from the street and the shop looks wider than the actual frontage size, a mere 10' 5". Inside, the traditional display window is replaced by a rotating conical stand with cut out recesses for exhibit-

ing objects. The sale of dresses is handled on this floor. Full height shelves units are designed with an oblique forward slant for easier reach by the sales personnel.

The mezzanine, obtained by utilizing the upper part of the original, lofty rooms, has a display and sales counter for accessories and also a stock room at the far end. Heavier clothing is sold in the basement, which also functions as fitting room by means of movable screens. All service fittings are hidden within curvilinear fixtures that give this room a stage-like character.

17 View from the street of the entire shop frontage. Note the conical display unit and the mezzanine floor above

18 Axonometric showing all levels. The rear rooms, at an angle with the main areas, are used for stock keeping, service and additional fitting space

19 Interior at ground level.
Note how the staircase gives
privacy to a fitting area
beyond, without loss of visual
depth

20 Looking up to the mezzanine
level from the ground floor

21 Detail of spiral staircase

A spiral staircase of cast concrete links all levels and includes display and service space wherever possible. The materials employed throughout are blue paint for walls and ceilings, a moss green velvety carpet that partially covers the walls. The furniture is chipboard, clear varnished and trimmed with black edging for the shelves, lacquered white for the conical display unit. Lighting is by articulated spotlights running on electrified tracks, with halogen bulbs. All items are designed by Sergio Asti.

22 One of the fitting areas
in the basement

Below
23 Looking up to the staircase
from the main room in basement.
Note fixtures, concealing
service fittings

Opposite
24 Overall view of main room in
basement. To the left can be
seen the mirror-faced movable
screens

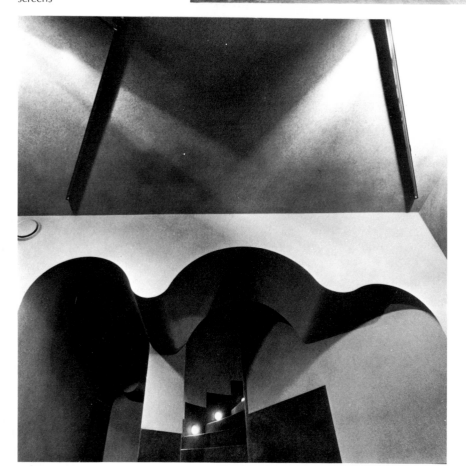

O-cha & Nori Kitamuraen: a Tea Shop in Tokyo, Japan

architect:
Katsuhiko Yamada

photography:
Eizaburo Hara

Before the comparatively recent development in building technology, the average lifespan of a Japanese house was about forty years. This was mainly because 'poor' materials were used, and house-building was essentially a craft; A few, sturdy wooden posts provided the frame, and sliding panels covered with rice paper defined the interior spaces. Yet, sophisticated joinery techniques allowed that, if necessary, the house could be knocked down and assembled again elsewhere. The simple shapes that could be obtained with limited resources became traditionally associated with Japanese design, and are still present in today's more industrialized buildings.

One such example is the shop where traditional Japanese foods – seaweed, tea – and also tea implements are sold. The modular design, the essential 'bareness', the colour scheme are typically Japanese, but materials and fittings are industrial ones. A long, rectangular room is lined on three sides with a black, wooden grid based on a cube – a shape symbolizing a tea chest perhaps, and repeated in the design of the sales counter and furniture. Some of these 'boxes' are drawers, some are fitted with shelves, others are backed with frosted glass concealing fluorescent lighting. The entire frontage is plate glass, the floor is lacquered carpeting. A most ingenious arrangement of lighting baffles on the ceiling uses expanded aluminium sheets in different sizes that partly conceal the ubiquitous spotlight and also act as diffusers. All wooden parts are painted black or white.

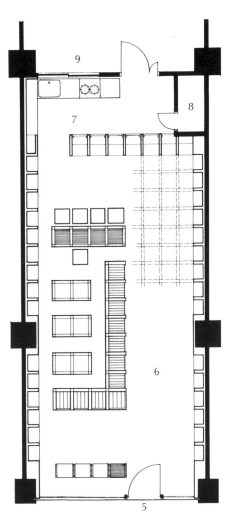

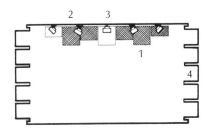

Left
25 Outside view

26 Section showing
lighting arrangement, and
floor plan

1 Lighting baffle
2 150 watt spotlight
3 100 watt spotlight
4 Display units
5 Shopping mall
6 Display area
7 Kitchen
8 wc
9 Storage area

27 Detail showing the special
lighting effect

Overpage
28 Overall impression of the
shop from the street. Note how
the different arrangement of
drawers and shelves avoids
monotony, and how the objects
displayed add interest to a
very formal design

29 The structural grid, 'grafted' onto the old wall. The entrance returns and the three upper slopes strengthen the frame; the web of the tee section is used facing out, to ensure watertightness. The frame was prefabricated and erected in sections at the site

'First of August' – a Boutique and Beauty Salon in New York City, USA

architect:
George Ranalli

photography:
George Cserna

This project is the renovation of a woman's dress shop in an old building on Lexington Avenue, New York City. The clients, who had occupied the ground floor premises for some years, were offered an option to acquire the first floor. They decided then to restructure the business both in volume and in scope; the old shop was to include one half of the new space and a beauty care salon would be installed in the other half.

Two considerations were given priority when the new design was discussed: firstly, the architecture should contribute in a positive, meaningful way to the life on the street in New York, avoiding the brash, commercial solution that relies on loud neon graphics. Secondly, the space should be open, with maximum exposure to the street and with the vertical circulation occurring in the front of the shop.

The analysis of the streetscape revealed that it was perfectly legitimate to extend the shop area to the limit of the original stoop. This possibility,

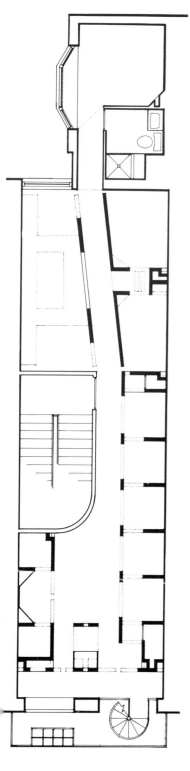

30 Floor plan; the second floor area measures 4·27 × 20·11m (14′ × 66′)

31 Lateral view, showing the architectural idea of 'layers'

and the desire for maximum visual openness, suggested a formula that expresses both a reinterpretation of the brownstone wall of the original building and the notion of the shop window. The grid kept reappearing as the most basic idea from which the architecture could be generated, and from this the design developed into three sectional 'layers' and a 'skin'.

The grid frame sets up a strong visual and structural order which moves across the surface and then is sliced at the top to deny the com-plete rigidity of that order; it can take on the properties of being solid or completely spatial in a few minutes, as the light of day changes or when it turns into evening; it is structural, therefore functions as a wall, yet does not disagree with the old wall – it is both the first 'layer' and the 'skin' of the architectural concept.

The second layer is the old brownstone wall. The thickness and mass of the wall have been maintained, and brought down to the ground. As one moves first through the grid to enter,

32 Entrance to the dress shop

33 Beginning of the beauty care salon, at the back of the shop, marked by a neon sign

34, 35 Detail of the beauty care
area and, below, the manicure
area, defined by a freestanding
wall with large openings cut in it

Opposite
36 another view of the manicure
area; light and colour are used
to identify spaces and their
specific function

then up the stair inside the grid space, it
becomes apparent that the large openings cut
into the wall signify that this wall must be
penetrated to reach the upper floor.
The third layer is a large green plane which is
attached to 'objects'; sometimes these are solid
forms, sometimes they define spaces: the
dressing rooms, the desk at the front, or the
dress rack spaces for example. At the end of
the dress rack a change of function takes
place, marked by a neon sign: this is the
beginning of the beauty care salon. Between
the second and third layer there is a small

Left
37 Interplay of surfaces and reflections in the dress shop area

38 Looking back towards the front of the shop

arrival space. It is narrow and thin, fitted with double mirrors, so that by standing at the top of the stair one sees the outside street moving by through the grid to an infinite horizon, and the interior, parallel with the street, also moves to infinity. This device allows the imagination to extend beyond the physical boundary of space, and recalls the function of the old mirrored waiting halls of Europe and America. The image at this point is of the three layers presented in infinity.

The Studio Home of the Architect in London, England

architect:
Stephen LeRoith

photography:
Richard Einzig

The London area between Kensington High Street and West Cromwell Road was fashionable among Victorian artists of the mid 19th century. Several studios were built there, in quiet cul-de-sacs off residential streets. At a later date, a group of six studios known as Stratford Studios were adapted for different purposes, including boat building, a stained glass workshop and a rehearsal space for a string orchestra. One of them was converted by architect Stephen LeRoith as his own home.

The original design used the ground floor as working space for the artist, with rest and cooking facilities, and the mezzanine gallery as a bedroom, completely enclosed. The space occupied by the main studio, about two thirds of the total area, had a full height, 17' ceiling with a mansard roof supported by two masonry walls at each end and by two intermediate trusses at 13' intervals. The north side of the roof was entirely glazed.

To preserve and enhance the spatial quality of the main studio the architect decided to retain the open plan arrangement in a flexible, informal way. Apart from the kitchen recess, spaces for living, dining and working are only defined by free-standing furniture, and can be interchangeable according to need. An existing

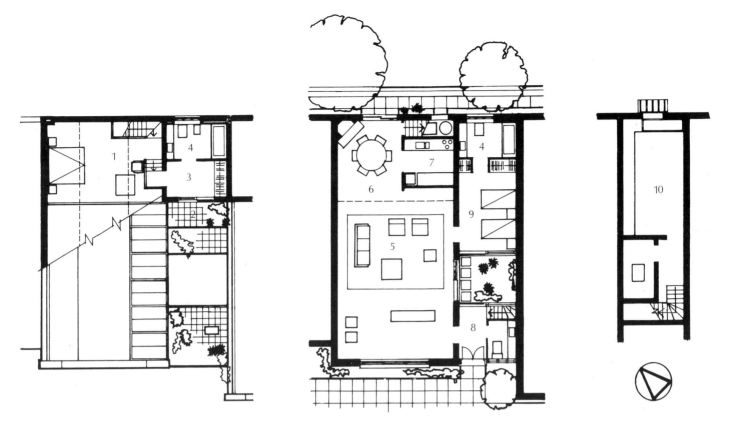

39 Outside view of Strafford
Studios. The street entrance
to the house is to the right

40 Plans

  1 Master bedroom
  2 Terrace
  3 Dressing room
  4 Bathroom
  5 Living area
  6 Dining area
  7 Kitchen
  8 Entrance Hall
  9 Bedroom
10 Darkroom/storage

41 A view from the entrance
hall; to the left is the
living area and across the
courtyard are the glass doors
to one of the bedrooms

Left
42 View of the open plan area, with the mezzanine gallery/ master bedroom

43 The open courtyard can be seen from many angles; here is a view from the living area

44 Another view of the ground floor space

45 Detail of the master bedroom

small kitchen has now become an open court with an attractive water garden, while the former living room has been converted into a second bedroom with adjoining bathroom.

The idea of the 8' × 10' water garden court came both from the need to provide light to the bedroom and to express the concept of relationship between exterior and interior spaces. The water is 4' deep, sufficient to grow a variety of marginal water plants in wicker baskets. The garden can be seen from the entrance, main studio and bedroom, and the reflections of glass and light complement the diffused north light from the glazed roof in the main open area.

The mezzanine gallery contains the master bedroom with adjacent dressing and bath

rooms. A roof garden outside the dressing room overlooks the water garden below.

All fittings were designed as simple framework of oak, with oak-veneered panels cut to identical widths and fixed with hinges to the framework, with $\frac{3}{4}$" reveals between the panels. The joinery is finished with matt polyurethane, which is heat and water resistant. The walls of the kitchen recess are lined with white plastic laminate.

The cellar is used as darkroom and for service equipment. Heating is by two independent hot air ducted units, with automatic humidifier; one is situated in the cellar, under the water garden court, the other is under the staircase to the main bedroom. The main studio area is heated from a series of perimeter registers.

46 View of the open court

47 Detail of open court with water garden

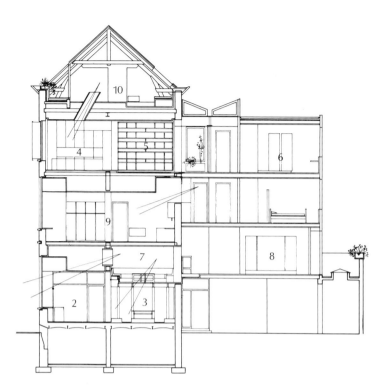

The Home of the Architect in Aalst, Belgium

architect:
Pieter de Bruyne

photography:
Gé Méijnen

A small, early 19th century terrace house was stripped of its original cladding during a conversion around 1950, and the delicate Neo-classical ornamentation of the facade was replaced by granite slabs. In 1974, Pieter de Bruyne remodelled the interior and designed an extension into the long and narrow back garden. He had two objectives in mind: to create areas with an individual atmosphere, intended for a precise, exclusive function, and to counteract the smallness of the house by visually disrupting the conventional idea of space. A study of the section will reveal the ingenuity of his approach. Rigorous economy of design uses all available space by changes in floor levels and use of integrated storage; mirror panels add visual depth; and a series of openings cut into floors and walls, sometimes even through specially designed pieces

of furniture, allows the passage of natural and artificial light to create new dimensions for the formal room shapes of the old house. It is here, in the original building, where the imagination has been spurred to the maximum.

A small, round mirror panel on the outside of the entrance door symbolizes the spatial manipulation to be found inside. From a small reception area one enters one of the front rooms, originally 4.29m high but now divided horizontally into a showroom, at the lower level, and a television room on the mezzanine above. The two spaces are visually connected through a round opening covered with glass in the ceiling of the showroom, and the floor joists of the upper level are left exposed. On the first floor are a study and the

48 Outside view; the alterations
to the original house, made in
1959, opened the way to the
changes carried out by Pieter
de Bruyne. Note the round mirror
panel on the front door and the
extension to a window belonging
to the blue room on the second
floor

49 Section showing the
position of the openings to
allow the passage of light and
the visual manipulation of space

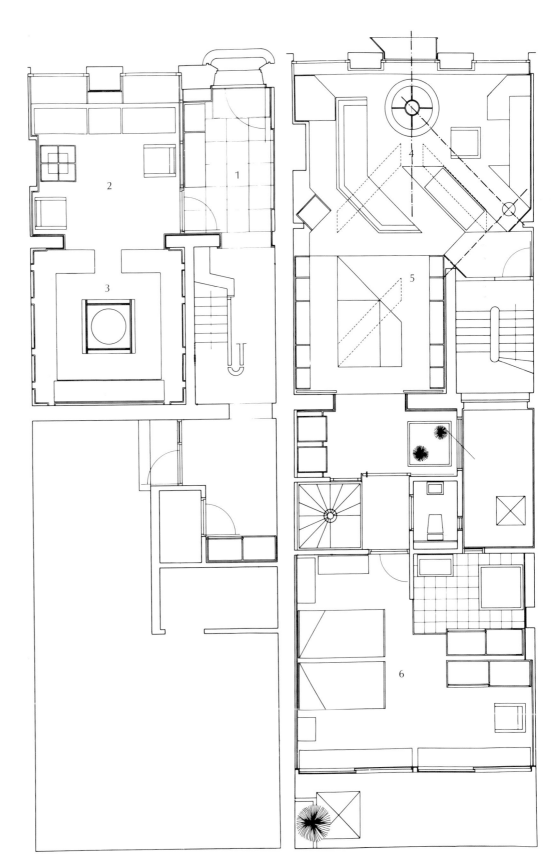

50 Plans of ground floor and
second floor

 1 Entrance hall
 2 Reception room
 3 Showroom
 4 Blue room
 5 Private studio
 6 Master bedroom
 7 Television room
 8 Dining area
 9 Office and studio
10 Guest room/recreation
    room

51 Showroom on ground floor; note the exposed floor joists of pine wood, belonging to the mezzanine where is the television room

52 Television room. The design of this space is based on the circle and the square – a formula preferred by the architect. Colours are in contrast with each other: red felt covers the walls, black leather for the round bench, grey for the carpet. The glass table is placed on a round opening in the floor, also covered with glass

53 The dining/kitchen room is adjacent to the television room. Walls are covered with white laminate, and the floor is lino. The dining furniture is a 1958 design by the architect

secretary's office. Walls and furniture are faced with white laminate and the study has built-in storage. The ceiling was lowered and three window embrasures have been retained. The actual windows have been altered into three horizontal sections: the lower and upper panels are fixed, and made of frosted and dark blue glass respectively; the middle section – the proper window – is fitted with Venetian blinds.

The second floor contains the blue room and the private studio of the architect. The blue room functions as a barrier between the busy street and the studio, and is used for relaxation and listening to music. This is

undoubtedly the most significant space in the house; all materials are in tones of blue, from the felt covering the walls, to the furniture, the carpet and the windows, fitted with dark blue glass. A shaft of light from the guest room above penetrates this room through a specially designed piece of furniture: it is the only natural daylight allowed into a sombre, introverted space. The private studio is open to the blue room and, at the other end, communicates by sliding doors with a subsidiary staircase in the new extension, a luminous space containing plants and the sound of water given by an artificial 'rain' falling on a glass dome.

54 The private studio of the architect is a windowless, secluded room adjacent to the blue room and opening, by sliding doors, to the transitional space between the house and the new rooms

55 The blue room, intended for relaxation and listening to music. All materials are in tones of blue: felt covers the walls, the windows are fitted with dark blue glass, carpet covers the floor and the plinths supporting the furniture, designed by the architect. The only natural daylight allowed in the room comes from the guest room above, through an opening in the ceiling. The light shaft falls onto the round table to the left

56 The 'nature' space that links old to new rooms. It is surmounted by a glass dome on which water is sprayed. To the right is the master bedroom, and a spiral staircase leads to the lower floors of the extension

57 The master bedroom and bathroom. The furniture of rosewood and walnut is by the architect and the bathroom walls are covered with Italian ceramic tiles by Fausto Melotti

The roof space has been fitted as a recreation area and guest room: brick walls and old beams have been restored and the roof has been insulated and finished with white laminate panels. The room opens onto a terrace – the flat roof of the new extension – so that one can enjoy nature as far as this is still possible in a town house. The whole atmosphere is in total contrast with that of the blue room, which can nevertheless be seen through the hollow, glass-covered white table.

By comparison, the new addition looks extremely simple. Function here seems to replace the intense, emotional symbolism of the old house. The transition is carried out naturally: there is an evident enjoyment of the freedom to express in the same idiom a concept that includes both architecture and furnishing. In every respect the architect has indeed succeeded in creating spaces that possess a character of their own, to suit many different moods and inclinations.

58, 59 Two views of the recreation room, also used as guest room. Note how the white panels lining the roof set off the exposed bricks and old beams. The specially designed white table to the left is hollow, with a glass top, to allow light to penetrate in the blue room below. The chair is by Gio Ponti

The Home of the Architect in Long Island, USA

architect:
Robert Stern

photography:
Carla de Benedetti

This shingle style house in East Hampton, Long Island, dates from 1900. In renovating the building the architect decided to retain some of the period character of the original, restricting the outside alterations to the addition of a new veranda to open up the inside of the house towards the garden. Although the new materials have been carefully matched to the existing ones, the design of the veranda makes no concessions to the original architecture, an intention underlined by the fact that the upper section of the veranda stands apart from the rest of the house.

The interior has been adapted to contemporary needs without changing the original layout: the ground floor is reserved for day activities and for entertaining, the first floor contains the sleeping area, and there are two extra bedrooms in the mansard roof space. All rooms have been painted white, an appropriate background to the architect's collection of modern paintings and objets d'art and to the furniture, mostly of contemporary Italian design. The only exceptions to the all white environment are the brick fireplaces in the living room and in the master bedroom on the first floor.

60 View from the garden; the
new veranda, left, is only
joined to the house at the
lower section. The whole
building is clad in cedar
shingles, with wooden fixtures
painted white

61 Plans

1 Entrance hall
2 Living room
3 Kitchen
4 Dining room
5 Reception
6 Master bedroom
7 Bedroom
8 Bathroom
9 Drawing room

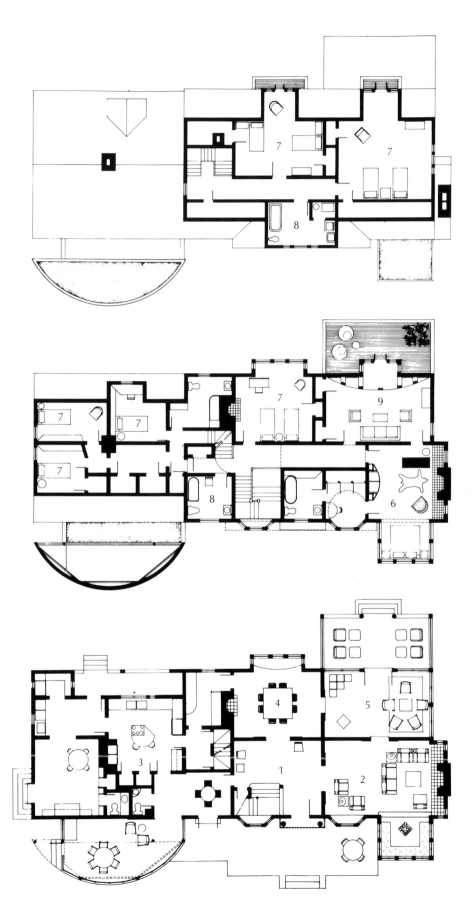

62 Reception room; the brick
coloured fireplace stands out
in an all-white environment.
The floor is also painted white

63 The formal dining room,
furnished with simple elegance

64 Detail of the kitchen, showing
the cooking unit in the centre
and walls fitted with cupboards

65, 66 Two views of the master
bedroom; the double bed fits
into the square alcove with
views over the garden. On the
opposite wall, behind the day
bed, is a painting by Peter Young

Overpage
67 Inside view of the veranda

68 The veranda, seen from the
main entrance

51

The Reception Rooms of the Commercial Bank of Copenhagen, Denmark

architect:
Ole Hagen

photography:
Lars Kaslov

The headquarters of the Commercial Bank of Copenhagen occupy a group of buildings erected between 1798 and 1888. The earlier of these, known as Erichsen's Palace, by the famous Niels Eigtved, is scheduled as a historical monument and protected in parts by a preservation order that only allows restoration work.

The architect Ole Hagen was therefore confronted with the problem of converting some interior spaces into modern bank premises, adapting the protected areas to modern use, and maintaining a certain continuity of style. It is fascinating to discover how this problem was solved. The part played by architecture was limited to a purely functional one, while the idiom of art and contemporary design was used as a link between past and present.

Grand, stately rooms for solemn functions have been left untouched; beautiful antique hangings and paintings acquire a new meaning in today's simple and luminous surroundings; pieces by contemporary Danish artists give character to completely new spaces. The transition is delicately balanced and effortless.

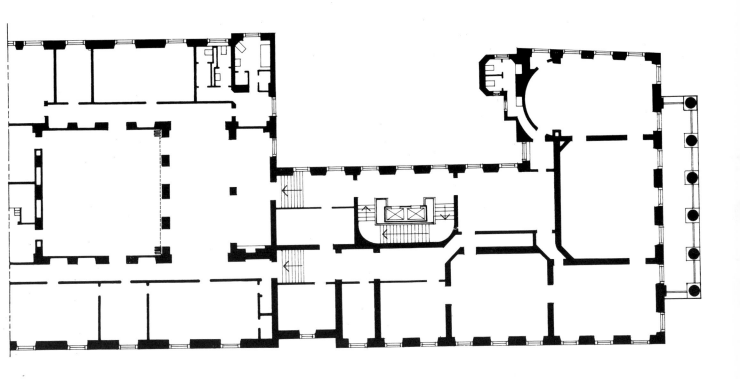

69 The Neo-Classic facade of Erichsen's Palace, now the headquarters of the Bank. The reception rooms are on the first floor

70 First floor plan

71 Main reception area in the Executive offices. The suspended wooden ceiling hides electrical fittings, the carpet is pale beige. On the walls are paintings by Mogens Andersen

Overpage
72 Another view of the main reception, showing the simple, functional approach adopted by the architect

73 One of the new spaces that contain contemporary works of art: a sculpture by Robert Jacobsen, at the far end, and, on the right wall, two hangings by the textile artist Jytte Gemzøe

74 A private function room for the Chairman to the Council of Management. Note how the antique hanging and painting and the contemporary furniture complement each other

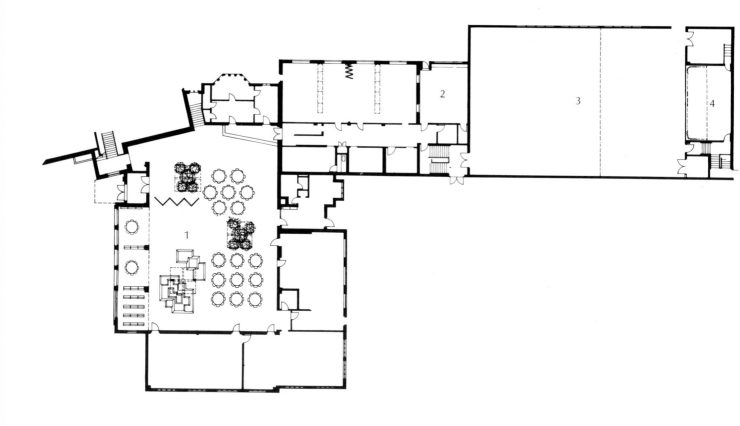

Renovation and Extension for a Community School at Ladue, Missouri, USA

architects:
Hellmuth, Obata &
Kassabaum

photography:
Barbara Martin

Progressive changes in the educational system of this private elementary school for 240 children created a need for more functional and flexible arrangement than was possible within the original building. An extension was indispensable, and also a better use of the existing multi-purpose room, where disparate activities such as theatre productions, library, indoor play and canteen had caused problems of space and organization. These were overcome by dividing the room into three main areas: the library/study, the lounge and the canteen.

The new addition, a double-height construc-

tion of yellow brick to match the existing building, has full length windows opening onto the park. Music gymnasium, theatre and science activities are now carried out there. All interior spaces have been re-designed with economy of means: sky lights abound, the open web steel joist ceiling and mechanical fixtures in the new building provide an anchor for gymnasium equipment. Paint, rather than architecture, creates the proscenium for the stage, while room dividers and multi-functional furniture afford maximum flexibility. Colourful graphics and banners create an atmosphere of lasting appeal.

75 Ground Plan

1 Multi-purpose room
2 Music centre
3 Theatre/Gymnasium
4 Stage

76, 77 The original building and
the new addition, as seen from
the 17-acres school grounds

78 Detail of the dining area in the multi-purpose room

79 View showing the well-defined arrangement of the renovated space: the library/study, left; the lounge, with the modular furniture in the centre; at the far end, the dining area

80 The theatre/gymnasium in the new building can be partitioned off for different kinds of activities

Overpage
81 Detail of stage proscenium

82, 83 The old premises shortly before being acquired by the architect (below), and the renovated building that is now the office of William Morgan

The Office of the Architect in Jacksonville, Florida, USA

architect:
William Morgan

photography:
Alexandre Georges and Ronald Thomas

The mellow red brick building that is now the office of William Morgan Architects was erected in 1902 shortly after a major fire disaster that hit Jacksonville. First occupiers were a blacksmith, whose workshop was in the smaller premises to the left, and a livery stable. Later, the entire ground floor was used as a parking garage and the first floor became a printer's shop and press. The original blacksmith's shop is now the entrance stairwell leading to the office on the first floor, while the ground floor serves as a garage for 19 cars and as an additional office space.

The renovation work is a remarkable example of simplicity and restraint. The external brick wall was sandblasted and restored; wooden columns, beams and sash window frames were retained and restored, and a new roof was provided. Contained within the original shell is the new structure – a neat white post and beam construction with plasterboard partitions. The main space at the lower level is taken by the reception area and by a meeting room; above this is an open plan drawing office, brightly lit by skylights cut between the exposed roof joists. The walls were painted white on three sides, the floor was carpeted and a heating and an air conditioning system was installed. The effect is of a strong, pleasant contrast between the rugged brick wall and the sleek white structure.

84 Plan of the office

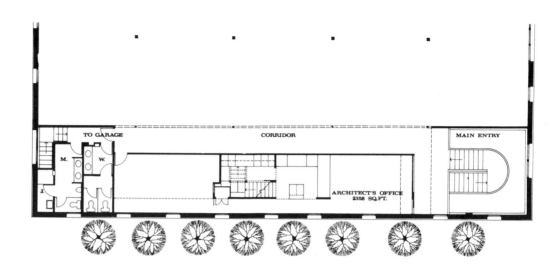

85 View of the reception area
and of the white structure
inserted in the old building

86 The drafting office on the
upper level

87 Looking towards the
reception area

Black Barn – A Family House at Frog Hollow, South Michigan, USA

architect:
Stanley Tigerman

photography:
Philip Turner

The client had acquired a 150-acre farm on which stood a hundred year old barn, built in the style known in the profession as 'Pennsylvanian Dutch'. The mansard roof was in a state of disrepair, but the interior structure of heavy, hand-hewn beams was in good condition, so the owner decided to convert the barn as a home for himself, his wife and their three children.

The architect's brief was based more on a sympathetic understanding of the existing structure, than on strictly functional considerations. However, as well as providing the usual family requirements, a studio for the lady of the house, who is a painter, and a music room that could contain a large theatre organ were needed. It was decided then to plan the whole interior as a series of galleries on different levels. The design utilizes the existing timber frame to support cedar veneer plywood panels that define the new spaces and also function as a bracing element. The different levels are served by a central helical staircase that continues up to the parents' bedroom under the mansard

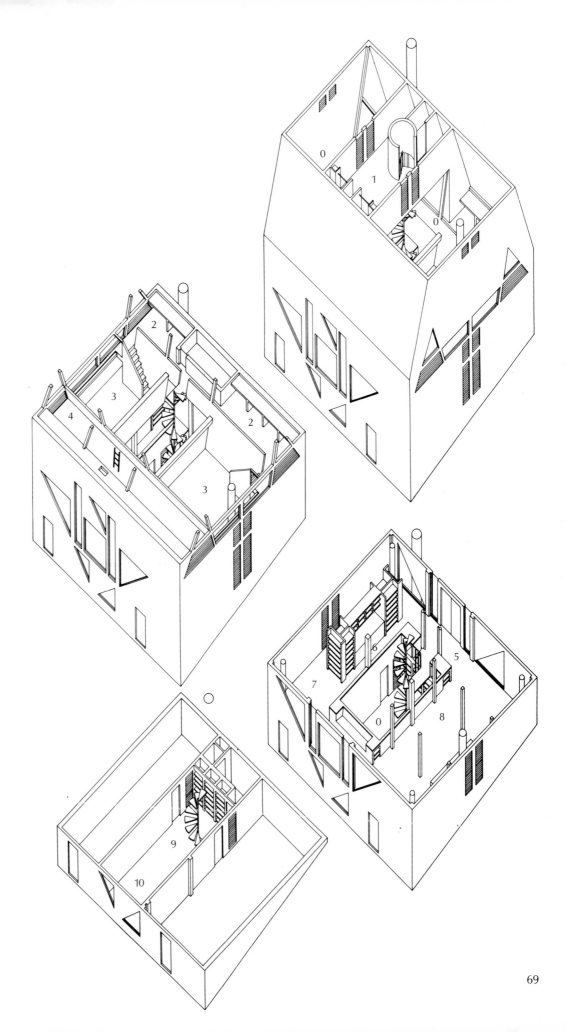

88 A wintry scene with the black silhouette of the house reflected in the nearby pond

89, 90 The old barn: before and after conversion. Note the attractive design of the windows

91 Axonometric

  0 Void
  1 Master bedroom
  2 Child study area
  3 Child bedroom
  4 Studio
  5 Entrance
  6 Kitchen
  7 Dining area
  8 Living area
  9 Study
10 Organ pit

Left
92 View showing the general layout of the galleries. The entrance door is at the centre back, the kitchen to the left and, to the right, is part of the living area. Main lighting is by means of huge globes hanging from the joists

93 View from the kitchen showing the music room below

root. This solution has many advantages: it retains the quality of the barn, provides well-defined, reasonably functional spaces and allows visual communication without the shortcomings of an open plan.

The entrance is at the first gallery level, where are living room, dining room and kitchen. The ground floor is used as a music and reading room. On the gallery above the living room is the children's area: bedrooms and a study, reached by a small flight of steps on a mezzanine level. Facing the children's area is the painter's studio and on the uppermost level is the parents' bedroom.

All conduits, heating ducts and plumbing are exposed and colour coded in blue, red and yellow respectively. The outside has been re-sheathed and then completely clad with black asphalt shingles. The attractive windows are fitted with grey tinted glass.

Left
94 Looking from the painter's studio to the children's bedroom and study area, and to the living room below

95 The studio, seen from the children's area

96 The parents' bedroom under the roof. The curved partition behind the bed conceals the top of the staircase

The Town House of the Architect in London, England

architect:
Alan Coles

photography:
Giovanna dal Magro

In a quiet mews off Portobello Road in
London, part of a 19th century stable, used
in more recent times as a builder's store, was
up for sale. The tiny two-storey structure
had a 4′ frontage and only one window, but
the singular shape of the space appealed to
architect Alan Coles, who decided to buy the
property and convert it into his own home.

The first consideration was, of course, space.
No permission to increase the height of the
roof could be obtained, yet the only way to
develop the floor area was to exploit the
space vertically. The architect gutted the

whole building; re-designed the roof, pitching
it at a more forward angle, and hinged the
entire house onto a structural brick pier that
passes through the highest roof point, on the
same principle as that of a tent. The whole
interior space could then be planned around
the central pier, from which branch off steel
joists to support the two timber upper floors.

Another problem concerned light. There were
no windows, or right to light, at the back
elevation of the house. So, a triangular tip
of the second level became a flat roof; from
this three skylights serve the floor below,

74

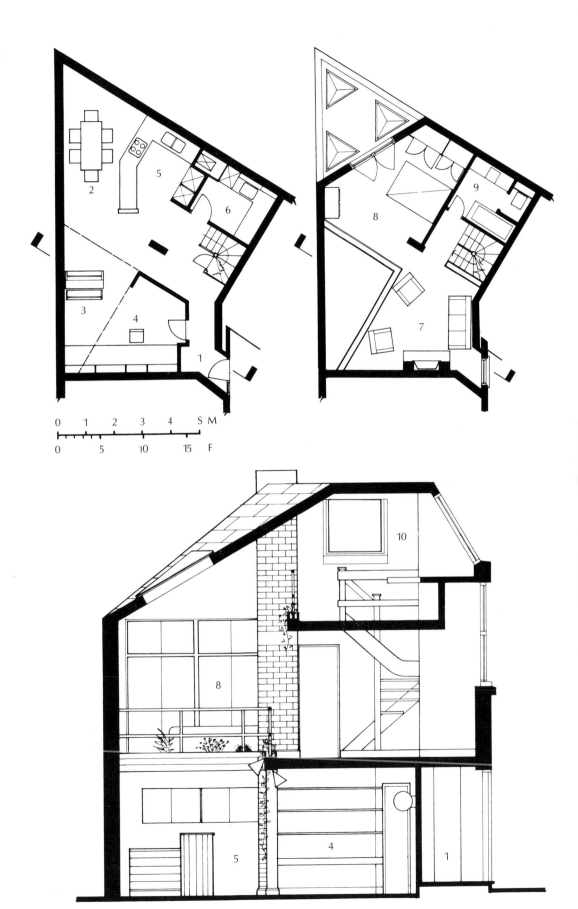

97 View of the converted mews; the entrance to the house is the small door in the centre of the picture

98 Plans and section of the conversion

1 Entrance Hall
2 Dining area
3 Music area
4 Study
5 Kitchen
6 Laundry and darkroom
7 Living area
8 Master bedroom
9 Bathroom
10 Gallery

99 View from the dining area; the pine counter to the left divides the kitchen from the dining area. Note the brick pier beyond and, in the background, the study corner

100 Looking upwards to the living/bedroom floor. Note the neat shelving and the lighting arrangement

Opposite
101 The living area, with the child's bedroom above, seen from the main bedroom

102 The bedroom opens onto a
tiny roof terrace punctured
by three skylights

and a double french window lightens the main
bedroom on the second level. Another window
was fitted to the front elevation of the main
roof. This scheme has completely transformed
the appearance of the interior: daylight now
pours from five openings in the roof and
contributes to the unusual spatial
characteristics of the different areas.

The ground floor has a brisk, practical
atmosphere. The entrance leads to a dining,
kitchen and service area on one side, with a
semi-enclosed study at the other. A handsome
dog-leg staircase of parana pine breaks
through the levels; on the first floor are

the living and sleeping areas, and the gallery
above is a versatile space with direct light
from three different angles that can be used
as a studio, workroom or second bedroom.

The finishing materials are simple and well-
balanced in texture: brown quarry tiles on the
ground floor, carpeting for the more relaxed
living and sleeping areas, pine for the gallery
floor. All walls are painted white, in contrast
with the exposed brick of the central pier.
Many green plants trail from the planters
around the void and fill the triangular roof
space outside the bedroom, giving an attractive
final touch to this remarkable project.

103 View of the living corner
from the stairs to the top level

104 A detail of the top floor

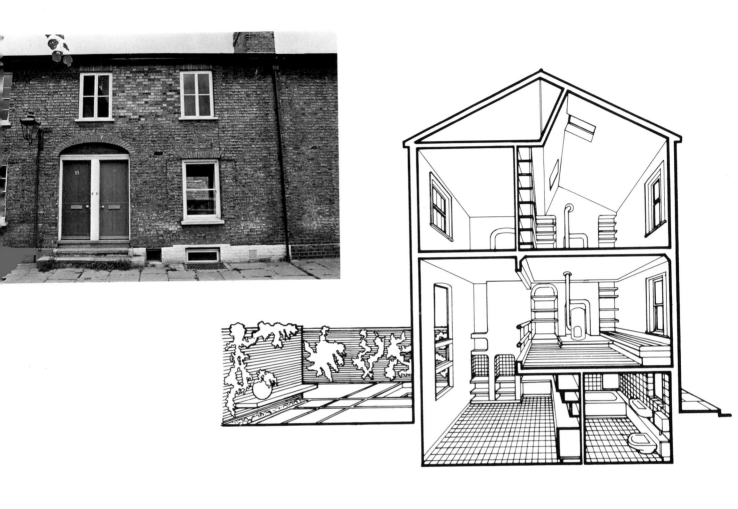

A Conversion at Willow Walk, Cambridge, England

architect:
Keith Garbett

photography:
Giovanna dal Magro

Willow Walk marks the southern boundary of a site known in the 18th century as Doll's Close. In 1810 an architect and builder, Charles Humfrey, bought and developed the site to a well-balanced plan consisting of 39 dwelling houses. Humfrey's scheme, protected today by a preservation order, is of particular interest to us both for being completely carried out by an architect who was a speculative builder and as an example of social town planning in early 19th century, the layout of the houses being clearly intended for two independent classes of society. Although the original green spaces have been filled by later additions, we can identify three types of original dwellings by studying the site plan. The more important houses, set well back from the road, are built on plots 46' wide; then we note the smaller ones at Short Street and Fair Street, and those at Willow Walk, only 16·6' wide, presumably intended for the staff of the wealthier class.

The present conversion is a remodelling of a modest house with two floors and a basement, realized with economy and meticulous care for detail. The basic structural changes are limited to demolishing a bathroom and to shifting the partition wall in the basement (see section). Yet

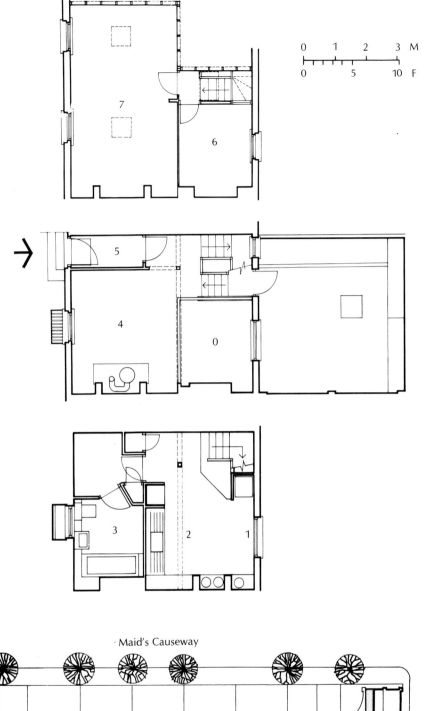

eft
105 Outside view; note how an
elliptical brick arch embraces
the entrance doors to two
different houses

106 Section drawing

107 Floor and site plans

0 Void
1 Dining area
2 Kitchen area
3 Bathroom
4 Living gallery
5 Entrance Hall
6 Bedroom
7 Study/Bedroom

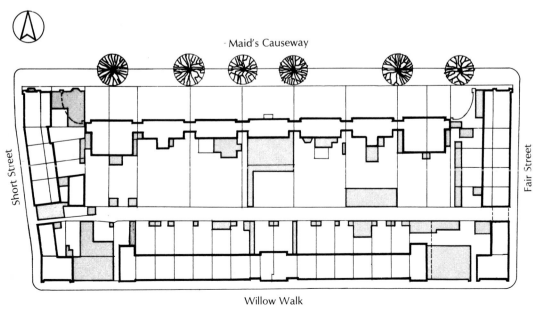

Doll's Close
(Conjectured original layout)

Reproduced by kind permission
of the Royal Commission on
Historical Monuments (England)

108, 109, 110 Three views of the
double height space obtained by
demolishing the former
bathroom.
Below: the living area over the
cooking/eating space; note how
the various recesses in the wall
add interest to and utilize all
available space. The other two
illustrations show a detail of
the cooking/dining corner and a
view of the working kitchen
space under the gallery

111 The living room on the
gallery, furnished with the
owner's collection of antique
pieces

112 Detail of the study/bedroom on the top floor

Opposite
113 Full view of the study/bed-room. Additional rooflights supplement the existing windows. Light plays an important role in this project

by comparison with the outside appearance, the improvement to the interior is astonishing. A small entrance hall with stairs to the upper and lower levels leads to the living room, now transformed into a gallery by the abolition of the former bathroom. A double height window cut into the north wall brightens the new space and opens the view to the garden, both from the basement and the gallery. The living area communicates with the dining space below, yet retains its intimacy through a well-thought furnishing design that focuses on a stainless steel Pither stove on an open earth. The kitchen/dining area is a bright, friendly space

simply decorated with white painted walls, yellow ceramic tiles and working surfaces of Westmoreland slate. Adjacent to the kitchen is an utility room and the bathroom.

The top floor contained originally three small bedrooms. The architect sacrificed one of them by demolishing the partition between the front rooms, facing south; then he raised the ceiling from the front elevation, along the roof line, and plunged it sharply to the original level under the highest roof point. This ingenious solution has produced an exciting space and completes an outstanding architectural idea.

The Country Home of the Architect near Paris, France

interior architect:
Alain Richard

photography:
Carla de Benedetti

The success of this project depends upon the strong character of the original buildings and on the unspoiled beauty of the countryside, on the border between Ile-de-France and Normandy. In the little Vexin village about 60km North-West of Paris two adjoining derelict buildings, former outhouses of a mill, were for sale. Alain Richard and his designer wife, quickly realizing the inherent possibilities of the site, decided to buy the property and convert it as their country home.

The buildings, set at right angles to each other, are in character with the other houses in the village. There is a small walled court-yard to the North-West end, and to the South a garden looks onto open meadows from which

it is separated by a stream. The architect's idea was therefore to emphasize the rural character of the old barns. He decided to retain the stone walls and the timber framework of the original structure, but to offset large volumes with small, intimate rooms; to open wide, full height windows that could be closed with big wooden shutters, and also small windows and dormers cut into the walls and roof so that there could be many different sources of light.

The building backing onto the road contains the garage, heating plant and the main entrance with staircase leading to the bedrooms on the upper floor. The other building, set well back from the road, includes two distinct areas: a full height living space, with large french

86

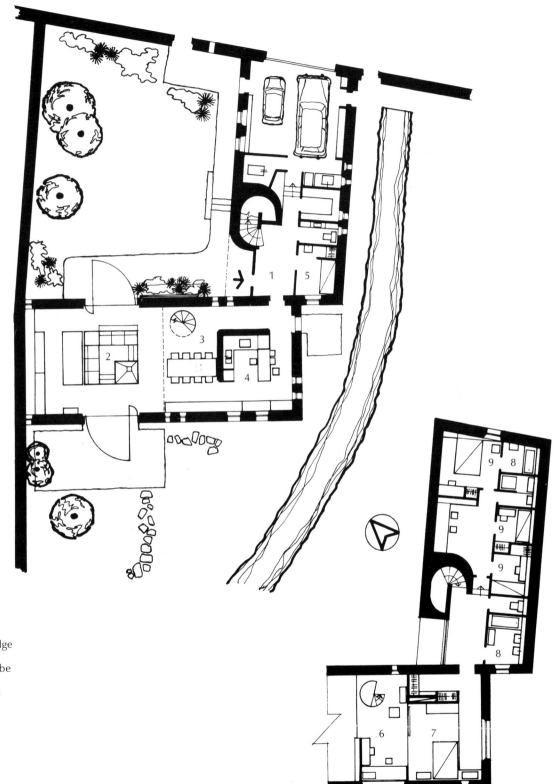

114 Looking from the open meadows across the foot-bridge to the west side of the house. Through the open doors can be seen the open hearth in the living area, and the courtyard below

115 Plans

1 Entrance hall
2 Conversation pit
3 Dining area
4 Kitchen
5 Guest bedroom
6 Study
7 Master bedroom
8 Bathroom
9 Bedroom

Left

116 The conversation pit as seen from the terrace outside. The brick floor continues inside and the seating bench around the hearth is on a stonework base

118 View of the dining corner under the gallery. The large table, normally set against the kitchen enclosure to the left can accommodate twelve people. It is of solid deal and was made by the local joiner

117 Dining/kitchen area and gallery as seen from the conversation corner. Note how the long cupboard, on its stonework base, links the kitchen with the dining room

Left
119 View of the study from the parents' bedroom in the gallery

120 Looking from the passage from the main entrance to the living area. To the left is the kitchen enclosure, in the centre is the spiral staircase to the gallery, the treads are painted black; at the back can be seen the conversation area

windows, and a more intimate area surmounted by a gallery. Under the gallery is the kitchen, contained within an L-shaped enclosure that terminates in a breakfast bar; still beneath the gallery, but merging with the more open living space, is the dining area. The whole floor is dominated by a square open fireplace with a black metal overmantel held in position by cables fixed to the beams. Around the raised hearth is a sunken conversation area.

The gallery, reached by a spiral staircase, is occupied by the parents' bedroom, dressing room and study/workspace. From the study a door communicates with the other building, where are the bathroom, children's bedrooms and play area. By closing this door and the

corresponding one on the ground floor, the two buildings could be made self-contained.

The interior finishes are very simple: only the new partitions are plastered and painted, the remaining walls are of fairface stonework. Most of the furniture, made by a local joiner, is of solid unvarnished deal that can be easily scrubbed clean. Cupboards are painted matt white or lacquered in gloss colours. The brick paviors used on parts of the outside are carried through into the living room; the upper floors are of natural beech covered by rugs. Lighting is provided by adjustable spotlights, designed by Allain Richard, and by diffused concealed lights.

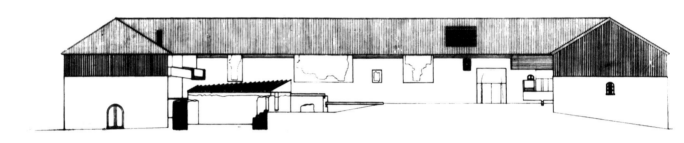

The Hamar Museum near Oslo, Norway

architect:
Sverre Fehn

photography:
Sjur Fedje, Truls Teigen

The Bishopric of Hamar, founded in 1152, was amalgamated with that of Oslo at the time of the Reformation and the buildings slowly fell into decay. Recent excavations revealed that the area is of great interest both to the archaeologist and to the historian; therefore the decision to build a museum for Hamar was based on the concept that the excavations are an important part of the museum itself, showing the visitor the very process of unravelling the path of ancient history.

In architectural terms the museum is 'suspended' over an area that includes the outbuildings of the medieval Bishop's Manor.

All existing walls and ruins have been left untouched, and a special storage arrangement occupying the entire basement can be seen through several openings from the museum, to give the public an idea of the total collection and of the continuous preservation work. The actual museum is on three levels connected by ramps that permit the visitor to be in contact with the archaeological excavations, both inside and around the new building.

At ground level the entrance ramp winds from the ancient farmyard up to the third level of the South Wing, where are a Lecture Hall for 200 people, built over the medieval barn, and

Left
121 External view of the Lecture
Hall within the walls of the old
barn, now the South Wing of the
museum

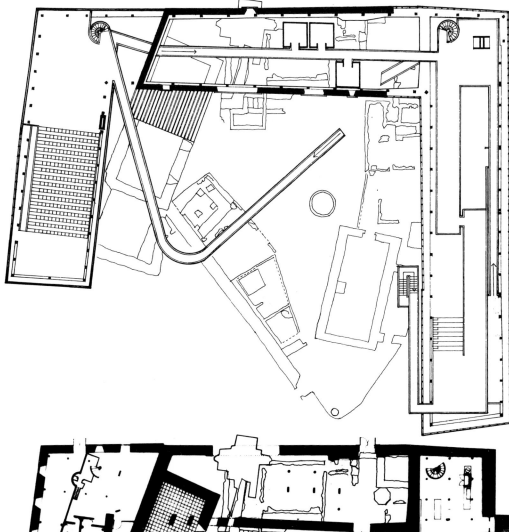

122 Sectional elevation from the
East. Note how the glass panels
protect and focus attention on
the damaged sections of the
original wall

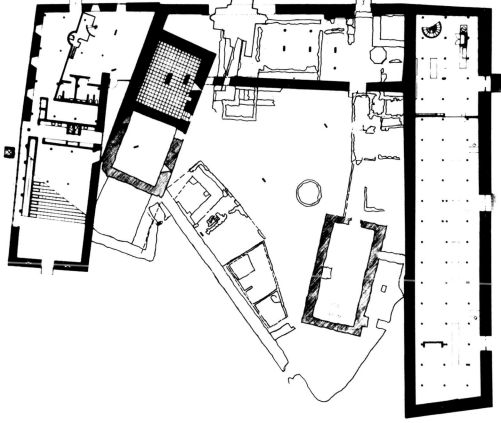

123 Plans of the first and third
levels showing the circulation
area of the museum

124 Outside view of the entrance
to the West Block

Opposite
125 View from the entrance hall:
to the right can be seen one of
the concrete pillars supporting
the entrance ramp which sweeps
past the glass door towards the
old farmyard area

the administrative offices. At the end of the
ramp a spiral staircase serves all levels and
links the Lecture Hall to the West Block, that
connects the South and the North Wings. This
is the real 'suspended' part of the museum: it
begins at second level as a ramp cantilevered
from a single row of concrete pillars, over the
exhibition area, leading up to the Folk Museum
at the third level of the North Wing, facing the
Lecture Hall. The entire West Block will be
devoted to the Middle Ages. From the centre
of the ramp it is possible to survey the whole
excavation area and to study from above the
process of exploration and discovery, to 'read'

the old foundations as if they were drawings
made of stone. Three small rooms built along
the ramp are for temporary exhibitions of
objects found during the excavations. The
Folk Museum will exhibit ethnic collections, in
particular those related to the history of grain
cultivation, transport, crafts, costume, from
pre-history to medieval times.

The materials employed in the new building,
concrete, wood, glass, contrast with the old
stones and at the same time complement them
with a subtle balance of texture and colour.

126 The Folk Museum at second level; looking West

127 The Folk Museum gallery, at third level

Opposite
128 Ramp leading from the second to the third level. Note, on both sides, the three small exhibition rooms

Left
129 The spiral staircase leading to the ramp, at second level, and to the Lecture Hall above

130, 131 Two views of the Lecture Hall: the West side and the sky-light arrangement, with the beautiful roof beams

132 External view from South-East. The glass cladding is of 6mm toughened glass painted grey on the inside and subsequently fired to obtain a corrosion-resistant finish

The Home of the Architect in Kensington, London, England

architect:
John Guest

photography:
Richard Einzig

This project is an interesting example of urban development in South Kensington, London. The architect's former home was a studio/house with a long back garden, occupying a site between two parallel streets. When the house became inadequate for the needs of their growing family, the architect and his wife decided to divide the property in half, sell the old house and, on the remaining half, build a new home. This solution was hampered by some opposition at first, but permission was eventually given subject to building constraints that, as is often the case, ended by having a positive influence on the final result.

Set well back from the road, the house appears as a single volume rising to the height of the neighbouring two-storey brick houses, dating from 1950. The precise, clean lines of the front elevation curve gently to the East to join the adjacent house and the entire wall is clad in grey glass, reflecting the surrounding houses and trees. A long, narrow opening glazed on two sides pierces the South-West corner of the house and introduces a change of rhythm that anticipates the change of mood occurring at the back of the house. Here the space is articulated in terraces and paved areas that begin half a level below street and are then repeated throughout the three floors. Reflections continue to play an important role as the glass cladding covers the back of the house and the garden wall, full height glass

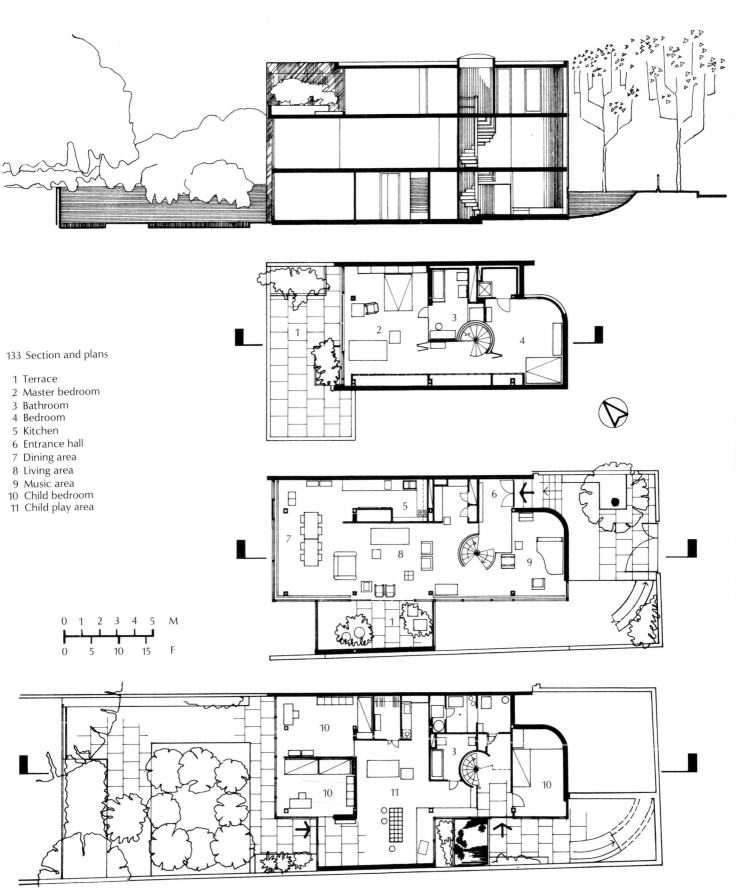

133 Section and plans

1 Terrace
2 Master bedroom
3 Bathroom
4 Bedroom
5 Kitchen
6 Entrance hall
7 Dining area
8 Living area
9 Music area
10 Child bedroom
11 Child play area

0 1 2 3 4 5 M
0 5 10 15 F

134 Main entrance at second
level. The staircase is surmounted
by a rooflight and was manu-
factured by John Desmond in
close cooperation with the
architect designer

Opposite
135 The playroom in the
children's zone on the first level.
The full-height sliding doors to
the left open onto a paved area
with a small pool. The garden
can be seen in the background

136 The living area on the second
level, above the children's zone.
The painting is by Mario Dubsky

137 Detail of the music area.
The grand piano is by Bechstein,
made in 1890

104

138 The South-West side of the house, with ramp leading to the children's zone

sliding doors provide direct access to the house from the garden, and a small square pool containing water plants occupies part of the open area that leads from the side to the street entrance, at the second level, by means of a curving ramp.

An atmosphere of spaciousness and light prevails inside. This is due to a combination of design and technical expertise. Reinforced concrete construction was chosen to obtain both clear uninterrupted spans and the possibility of building on three floors within the height of the two-storey surrounding houses. The frame rests on a concrete pad foundation; 200mm concrete block was used for external, 100mm for internal walls. Floors

are easily maintained white ceramic tiles from Italy, with some areas of 'Norament' rubber tiles on courtyard and in the playroom. The roofs are asphalt on reinforced concrete. All door and window frames are aluminium. The attractive spiral staircase linking the three levels, also of aluminium, is a design by the architect realized in close co-operation with the manufacturer.

Heating is provided by two gas-fired boilers, one supplying a ducted warm air system and the other perimeter units situated beneath the windows. The furniture, with the exception of the aluminium terrace chairs designed in the thirties by Hans Coray, is mostly of Italian design.

139 The master bedroom and
the terrace on the third level

140 Looking towards the bathroom and the top landing of the
staircase from the master
bedroom

Opposite
141 View of the spiral staircase
through the rooflight

142 Axonometric showing the relationship between the new interior and the original shell

Opposite
143 Plans of the four levels

 0 Void
 1 Entrance hall
 2 Whig administration
 3 Reception
 4 Lounge
 5 Exhibition
 6 Terrace
 7 Office
 8 Multi-media room
 9 Debate panel office
10 Seminar room
11 Balcony
12 Projection room
13 James Madison room

144 Whig Hall, from the main avenue

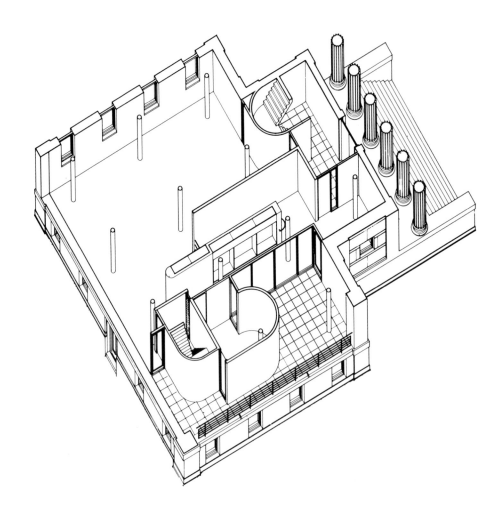

The New Whig Hall at Princeton University, USA

Whig Hall, base of the Whig Debating Society, was one of two identical buildings in the 19th century eclectic style, designed as part of a complex on Princeton University campus. The reconstruction of the Hall was decided after an outbreak of fire that destroyed all but the shell of the building. It was then agreed that the new interior should be opened to general university use as well as fulfilling its original purpose. This meant that 3,000 sq.ft. of new space had to be added to the 7,000 sq.ft. of the former structure, and that the Hall would be used for several, possibly conflicting, activities. There was to be an information centre; university

work-room and lounge area; seminar rooms; a flexible meeting space for debates, lectures, receptions; offices and projection facilities.

The different nature of the new activities posed some planning difficulties. The privacy and compactness of the Debating Society spaces had to be retained, while the more public areas needed to be inviting enough to encourage student participation; hence the special attention given to the circulation area (see axonometric drawing and plans).

On the following pages an attempt has been

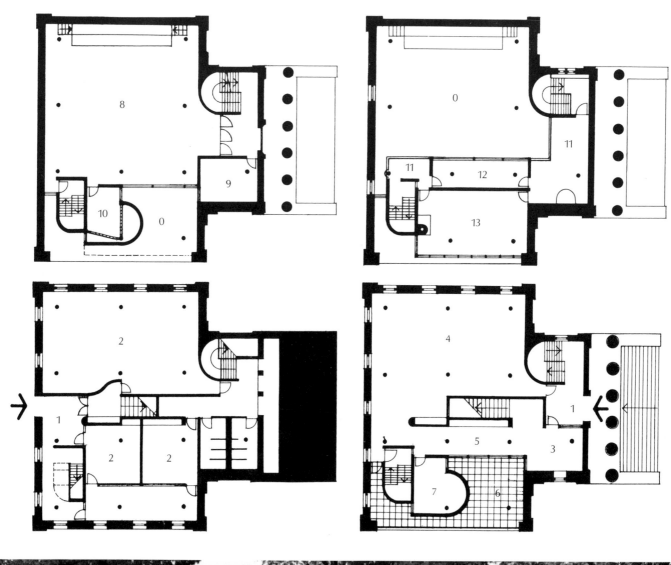

145 Looking upwards from the North-West corner to the seminar room at second level

146 View from the glazed entrance hall

Opposite
147 Part of the western facade showing clearly the concept of using the old shell as a container for the new building. The use of contrasting materials strengthens the design idea; the new 'object' within the marble faced brick bearing walls is of concrete block construction, with stucco finish outside and inside

made to illustrate the aesthetic qualities of this project. A respect for the original building, in the context of architectural history, interpretation of the concept of tradition, and relationship with the existing complex, led to the design idea of an object within a container. The new building, embodying the clarity of the original single volume, is contained and at the same time revealed by the marble shell. As an example of modern concept of architectural space, within the formal base, column and cornice elements of the eclectic style, Whig Hall symbolizes the passing of time and, on a different plane, exposes the inadequacies of that style.

148 Overall view of the West
elevation of the Hall

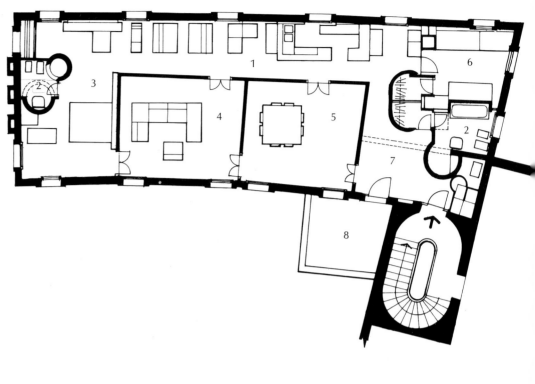

An Apartment in Palazzo Erizzo, Venice, Italy

architects:
Valeriano and Michelina
Pastor

photography:
Aldo Ballo

From this apartment on the top floor of the Palazzo Erizzo in Venice, 20 metres above water level, the unimpeded vista of the city and lagoon ranges over 360°. This was to be the main determining factor in the work of renovation undertaken by the architects.

The original layout consisted of a series of intercommunicating rooms, some small, with two and three doors; this restricted both freedom of circulation and the amount of useful space. The architects decided to

demolish the partitions between the small rooms and from the space thus obtained they created a long gallery from which one enjoys views of the unique city as an uninterrupted sequence through the original openings, now converted into picture windows. The gallery ends with a small internal veranda looking towards the distant church of the 'Salute', an incomparable focal point. The new area has become the living space of this home; easily maintained, it has specially designed furniture to define a small kitchen of white laminate, and

a living area adjoining the bedroom to the left.

The unusual finish on the walls and ceiling of
the gallery needs special mention because it
is based on a local traditional technique known
as 'calce rasata'. A layer of plaster containing
only slaked lime and clean river sand – with
no trace of cement, hydraulic lime or chalk –
is first applied to the brick wall. When the
plaster has dried out the finishing process
can begin. The area is divided into panels –
each to be treated separately – and a
compound of paste of slaked lime, with small
quantities of synthetic adhesive and soap
flakes mixed to a thick, smooth, frothy
consistency is brushed on and then worked
well onto the surface with a special tool,
a flat iron called a 'fratazzo', which is
pressed against and drawn across the surface.
This process is repeated several times until
the characteristic texture and translucency
of the finish is obtained. The addition of
special pigments, oxides, or other synthetic
materials to the basic mixture produces

154 Part of the bedroom, to
the left, and full height
cylindrical 'containers'

Opposite
155 View of the small veranda
from the living area

Overpage
156 A corner of the drawing
room, simply furnished to
enhance the original 17th
century decoration

157 Another view of the
entrance hall, from the
dining/reception room

coloured surfaces of delicate brilliance and
transparency, reminiscent of water-colours.
White was chosen in this case, to enhance
the colourful views of the outside; the
changing daylight gives these surfaces a
mother-of-pearl sheen.

The two largest rooms, adorned with valuable
stuccoes and painted ceilings dating from the
17th century, have been carefully restored
and are used for entertaining on more formal
occasions. Spotlights and contemporary
furniture, used in conjunction with antique
pieces, do not disturb or detract in any way
from the magnificence of these rooms.

The services have been planned within two
groups of free-standing cylindrical volumes,
acting as functional 'containers'. The
largest of these is located in the wide
entrance area and includes the bathroom,
dressing room, heating installations and so
on; a smaller group occupies part of the
bedroom space and is lit by a glazed partition
in the veranda. All original floors, in the
technique known as 'alla veneziana', have
been restored, along with the original stuccoes,
frescoes and lacquers, by a small team of
highly specialized craftsmen still available,
though sadly not for very long.

Instruments for Early Music by Today's Makers

by Fiona Adamczewski

158 Jaap Bolink working on a violin in his workshop in Hilversum, Holland. Son of a violin-maker, he made his first instrument in 1959

An interesting anachronism which emerges as soon as one attempts an assessment of the situation in current musical instrument construction is that, in an era which has produced Concorde, the most vital work being done in the field of musical instruments is concentrated on the production of instruments for the performance of what we loosely term 'early music'. One could argue that music which takes its place in an analogy with Concorde has nothing whatsoever to do with theorboes, racketts or sackbutts. The atonal compositions of Stockhausen require the human voice and electronic processing of live sound in real time. If we are presented with a potentiometer do we recognize it as a 'musical instrument'? And here we run into our first difficulty. Perhaps it is only a semantic one – but it presents us with the unavoidable necessity of selection.

'Instruments are devices for provoking vibrations in the air, which vibrations impinging on the drum of the ear, create a nervous disturbance which we call sound.' Thus the Oxford Dictionary of Music. The Oxford Dictionary itself defines an instrument as 'a contrivance for producing musical sounds'. Given these definitions we can neither exclude a comb wrapped in paper or, at the other end of the scale, a ring-modulator. Depending upon the receptive ear, either might be said to be the source of a 'musical sound'. Faced with a comb we think of hair and faced with a ring-modulator most of us would simply be perplexed; but then again many of us might be equally perplexed when presented with some of the rarer forms of medieval instruments. On the other hand, confronted by a 'cello or a flute we are left in no doubt that what we perceive before us is indeed a 'musical instrument'. For the purpose of an introduction such as this it will be necessary therefore to limit the definition of a musical instrument rather strictly, and I shall consign the electronic category to a position beside computers and the ultra-sound devices of contemporary medicine.

I am left therefore with three classes of instruments: stringed instruments, which can be sub-classified into those that are plucked and those that require the friction of a bow; wind instruments, with again a sub-classification as to whether the air in the instrument is set in motion by simply blowing into a tube, with or without a mouthpiece, blowing through a reed or blowing through the lips, which then serve as a reed, as for example in the case of brass instruments with again a sub-classification as to whether the pitch is determinate or indeterminate. It is when one comes to look at what is happening in the construction of instruments falling into these categories that the bias in the direction of early instruments emerges. Seeking for the reasons for this situation we have to consider the musical climate as a whole.

Looking back fifteen years at a record catalogue one is struck by the fact that comparatively few recordings of early music existed then. Today the situation is dramatically different; the music of Monteverdi, of Dufay and Josquin is familiar to a very much larger audience than hitherto. Musical audiences are able to attend concerts of Renaissance and medieval music with increasing frequency. Fifteen years ago very few early music consorts existed and there were relatively few instrument makers concentrating on the production of instruments for the performance of early music. Looking at the picture in 1977, when new early music consorts are springing up continually, one is intrigued to discover the reasons for the change.

To understand fully the complicated reasons for this 20th century revival of interest in medievalism, it would be desirable to consider in detail the historical and sociological background of the 19th and 20th centuries. This is

159 Two alto shawms; the shawm, a forerunner of the oboe, was played in Europe up to the first half of the 17th century; maple wood with the bell section cut from the solid, in the traditional manner, and brass keys and decoration

160 Full consort of shawms; from left to right: great bass, bass, basset, nicolo, alto, treble descant; these instruments derive from original, playing specimens held in collections at Brussels, Berlin, Vienna, Prague, Nuremberg – with one exception: the descant is based on a description of the Klein Schalmey from the 'Syntagma Musicum' by Michael Praetorious, published by Wolfenbüttel between 1615 and 1619; heights range between 50cm and nearly 3m

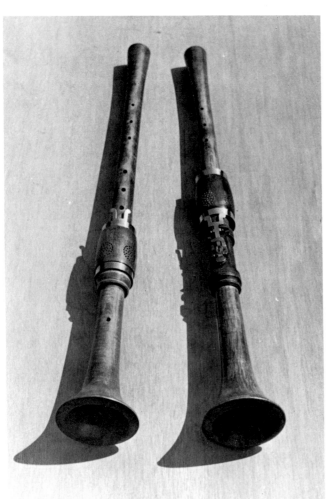

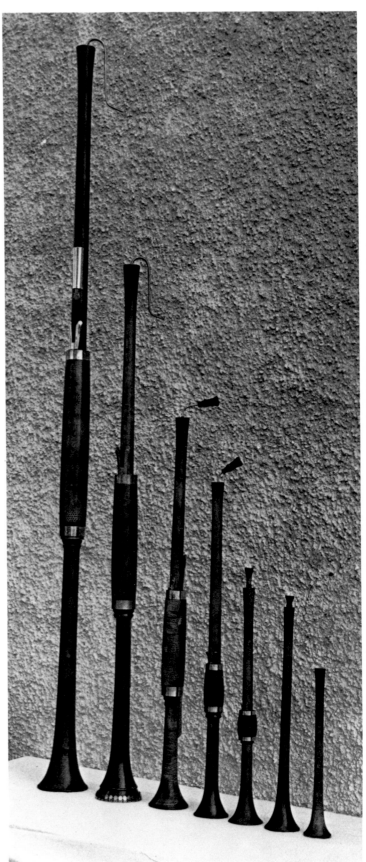

161 Renaissance bass rackett;
the rackett, used in the Middle
Ages and the Renaissance, is
a deep-toned, double-reeded
instrument of cylindrical bore;
a short, solid cylinder of dense
wood or ivory is bored through
its length with a number of
cylindrical channels which are
then connected in such a way
as to form a single, long,
narrow tube; the illustration
shows an ivory copy of the only
known surviving exemplar held
in the instrument collection at
the Karl Marx University, Leipzig

162 Consort of crumhorns; a
double-reeded instrument, the
crumhorn was popular between
the 15th and 17th centuries; the
illustration shows, from left to
right, a bass, tenor, alto and
soprano, all copies of original
instruments held in the
Conservatorium at Brussels

All instruments illustrated on
these two pages were made
by John Hanchet, England,
between 1965 and 1977

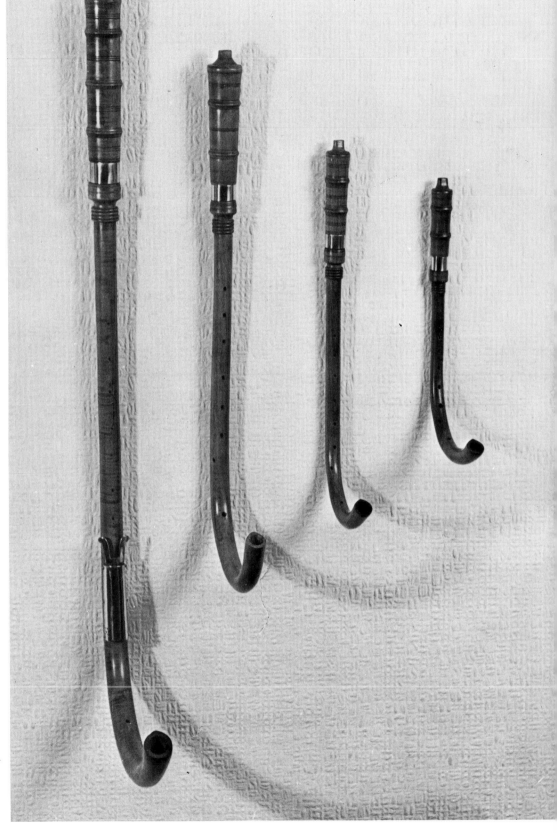

163 Tambours; based upon the earliest and simplest form of drum; laminated plywood frames, vellum skins; the decoration is woodburnt, painted with stains and natural pigments, then polished with beeswax; cm 35Ø × 10cm high (14″ × 4″). Made by Lynn Fisher, England

scarcely the place for such an analysis, but it seems likely that the roots of this revival of interest may lie, somewhat paradoxically, in the rapid growth of technology and the consequent development of communications systems during this century. An international musical language has gradually developed to serve the international community which was formed by the industrial revolution of the 19th century. It is possible to trace the source of this 'language' to the 19th century pre-

occupation with Empire building. Contact with alien cultures, the ancient civilizations of China and India, no less than the undeveloped areas of Africa, brought Europe into contact with a wealth of alien forms of art and music. Composers, intrigued by the music of unfamiliar cultures, demanded the adaptation of many instruments from 'primitive' musical traditions, and the influence of 'primitive' music on our own resulted in a new attitude to rhythm and harmony.

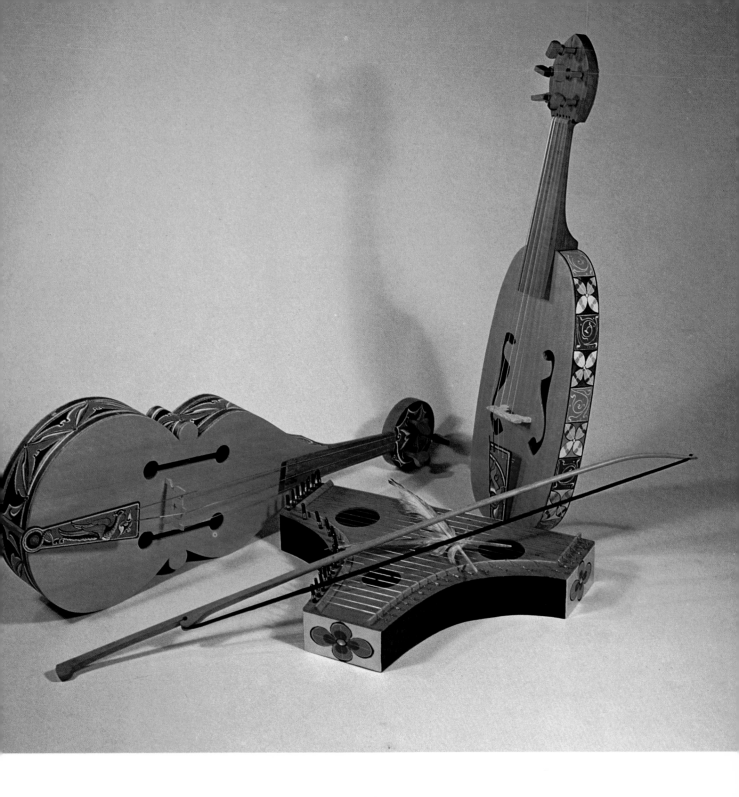

164 Medieval viol, fythele and psaltery; these instruments were favoured by itinerant musicians throughout the Middle Ages and appear in numerous paintings up to the Baroque period; the examples illustrated are made of many woods: sycamore, Swiss pine, English yew, cedar, cherry, and beech for the bow; gold leaf and tempera decoration, based on medieval manuscript paintings; the viol is 81·3cm (32″) the fytele 68·5 (27″) long, the psaltery is 35·5cm × 40·6cm (14″ × 16″); the bow is 89cm (35″) long
Made by Christopher Allworth, Canada

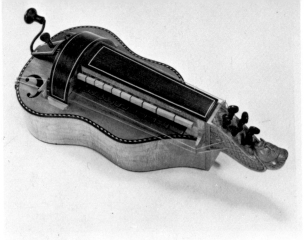

165 Clavicytherium; instruments of this type, with vertical sound-boards, were built very early in the history of the harpsichord; an illustration of one appears in a dialogue on musical instruments, 'Musica Getutscht', written by a German priest, Sebastian Virdung, in 1511; the illustration shows a clavi-cytherium based on an original instrument circa 1480 in the possession of The Royal College of Music, London
Made by Derek Adlam, England

166 Hurdy-gurdy; a popular instrument in the Middle Ages; a rosined wheel turned by the left hand serves as a bow, while the left hand plays the notes on a small keyboard
Made by John Nicholson, England

167 Psaltery; widely known in the 14th and 15th centuries, the psaltery resembles a dulcimer but is played by plucking with a plectrum or the fingers
Made by John Nicholson, England

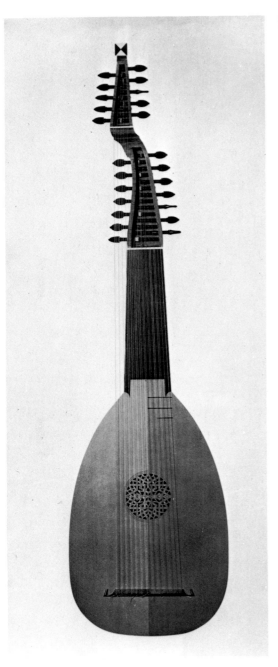

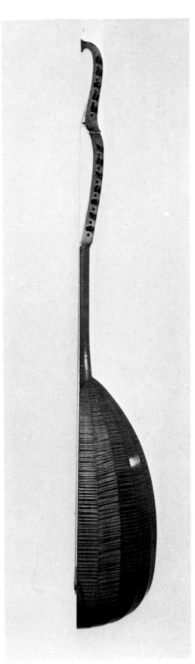

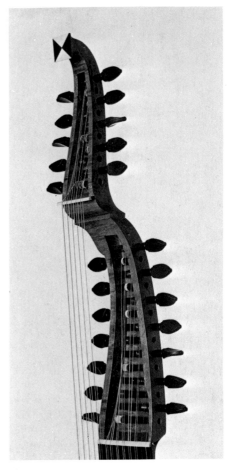

168, 169, 170 Thirteen-course
Theorbo; the peculiarity of
this instrument, of the lute
family, is the double peg-box,
the set of strings attached to
one box passing near a fingerboard and those attached to the
other being left free, to be
plucked as 'open' strings (see
detail); the body is figured
sycamore, the soundboard is
spruce and the neck and peg-
boxes are carved from one piece
of bird's eye maple
Made by Ian Harwood and
John Isaacs, England

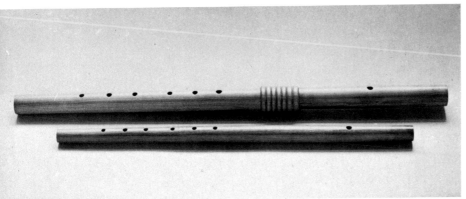

171 Renaissance flutes; these
instruments are made with the
typical small embouchure of the
time; the tone is louder and
coarser than that of the modern
flute
Made by John Cousen, England

172 Treble Rebec; the fore-
runner of the violin, the rebec
probably derived from the Arab
'Rabab' and was very popular
during the Middle Ages and the
Renaissance
Made by John Nicholson,
England

173 Portative Organ; this earliest
type of organ was frequently
carried in processions; St.
Cecilia, the Patron of Music, is
often depicted playing one; the
keyboard is manipulated by one
hand while the other hand
operates the bellows
Made by John Nicholson,
England

174 Group of Cornetts;
references to the cornett are
found as early as the 10th
century and its use is
recommended in directions for
Shakespeare's plays
Made by Christopher Monk,
England

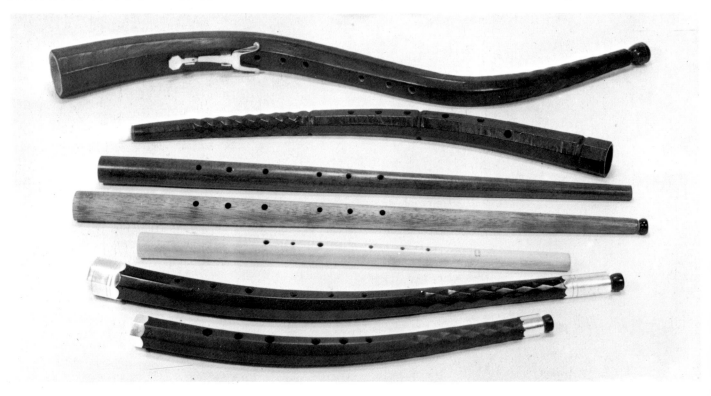

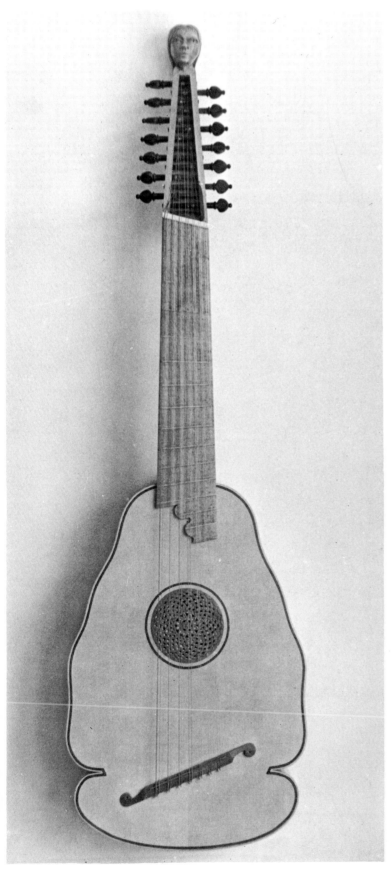
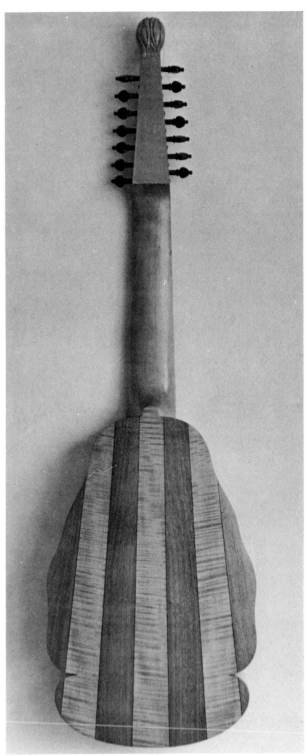

175, 176 Bandora; played with
a plectrum, the bandora was in
use until the end of the 16th
century; this example is of
sycamore and walnut, with brass
and steel strings and rosewood
pegs
Made by P. Forrester, England

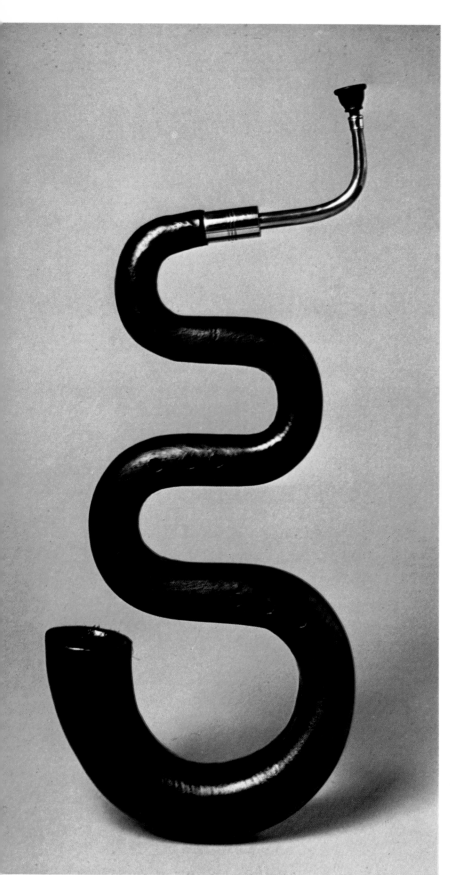

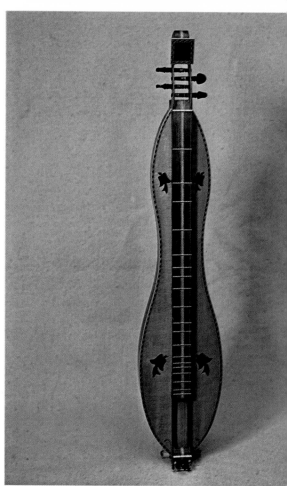

Two world wars in the 20th century have destroyed these old empires and served as a stimulus to the advance of technology. The years between the two world wars were notable for the reactions of anger and despair manifested both in Europe and in the United States of America. The twenties brought prohibition to America, inflation to Germany and disillusionment to Britain, and in 1929 the Wall Street Stock Market crash affected the whole world. Unemployment was manifest and a swing to communism united both workers and intellectuals in the thirties. The second half of the 20th century has seen the emergence of the media as an instrument of persuasion, and perhaps the most paradoxical aspect of progress is the international standardization of tastes and attitudes.

Today's traveller, rushing to catch his jet flight, exchanges one city complex for another with little possibility of losing in the process the sight of blue jeans, Coca-Cola advertisements, multi-storey buildings, multi-lane highways, radio-taxis or television screens. Newscasters may speak different languages, but they offer international news. Today's musician may live in Finland, but through the agency of super-sonic flight his programme may demand that he perform in Hong Kong, New York and Rome in the space of a week.

The world of Lorenzo de' Medici seems to us, despite its intrigues and physical dangers, a very simple and restful world by comparison. And perhaps this is where the appeal of medievalism lies; and also its dangers. Could we perhaps find the key to the present revival of interest in early music and instrument building in a nostalgia for that more personal-ized world where things were, of necessity, hand-made and life demanded another time scale, and respect for the individual. One might argue that 20th century composers and performers coming to terms with their specialized science-dominated world would seem to require an informed acquaintance with mathematics and electronics. Inevitably the music they produce is regarded by the majority of people as 'difficult'; but to Beethoven's contemporaries his last quartets were probably 'difficult' too. In Baroque music tonality is essentially stable and perhaps that is what some individuals seek. Tranquillity, in any event, is undoubtedly difficult to find in our noisy machine-dominated world. I am amused sometimes to find that in a workshop where a young craftsman is reconstructing a

181 Renaissance Tenor Recorder; the recorder was immensely popular and frequent references to it occurred in English literature of the 16th and 17th centuries. Henry VIII was a recorder player and possessed 76 recorders. An important instrument also for ensemble playing, the extent of its family range allowing it to be used in sets of three, four or five of different sizes. The sound is produced on the same principle as that of the organ pipe; this example is of acid-stained boxwood
Made by John Cousen, England

182 Baroque Tenor Recorder; this instrument differs from its earlier prototype in one significant detail: it has a narrower, more steeply conical bore giving a distinctive tone colour. Built in three joints of rosewood, with brass keys
Made by Arnold Dolmetsch Ltd, England

183 Polygonal Virginal based on an instrument by Marco Jadra (1952) kept at the Pitt-Rivers Museum, Oxford. The construction is extremely light, with the bridge and nut on the soundboard to produce a good bold tone 1·61m × 48cm (63¼″ × 18¾″)
Made by Denzil Wraight, England

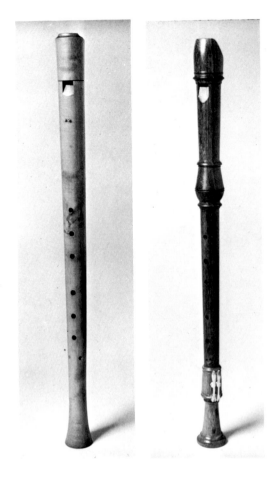

rebec, a transistor radio is playing the latest rock music. The answers, I must conclude, are not quite so easy.

Undeniably the world of the seventies is one in which we are battered by a thousand stimuli and confused by the growing necessity to push the frontiers of our knowledge further and further. Renaissance man lived in a humanistic climate where he could be reasonably certain that he was acquainted with all the elements that constituted his civilization. This is certainly not the case with us. Threatened by a loss of identity and confused by the complex intellectual world we inhabit, we are forced more and more towards specialization. We see about us indications of a growing disinclination to accept the packaged life that seems the natural ambience of 20th century man. Time and history may clarify the matter, but for the moment perhaps it is more pertinent to consider the individuals who have contributed to the growth of interest and the revival of involvement in the performance of early music and the consequent demand for the authentic instruments for its performance.

It is very difficult to accurately attribute the credit for the rebirth of interest in early music and its performance on reasonably authentic instruments. Certainly it seems likely that two names appear at the top of the list, those of Wanda Landowska and Arnold Dolmetsch. The 1890s saw the emergence of both.

Arnold Dolmetsch, then a young French music teacher working in London, presented a concert of early music performed by his pupils on strings and a Shudi harpsichord lent by Broadwoods in 1890. Dolmetsch had developed a love for early music during his student days at Brussels Conservatoire, where he and his fellow students were able to borrow viols from the Instrumental Museum. He began at this time to amass a personal collection of musical instruments and in 1894 he made his first clavichord, followed two years later by his first harpsichord. In 1902 Dolmetsch made a tour of the United States presenting early music played on early instruments and this resulted in an invitation from the Boston piano makers, Chickering and Son, to set up a department for the production of harpsichords, clavichords,

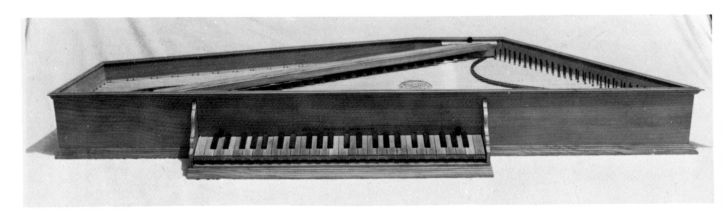

184, 185 Six-course cittern; a wire-stringed instrument of great antiquity, the cittern was played with a plectrum until the end of the 16th century, when the use of fingers was encouraged for improved tone. It was very popular in Shakespeare's times, when it was to be found in barber shops for the amusement of waiting customers. The example illustrated is of English figured sycamore with a soundboard of spruce; boxwood and satinwood fingerboard and pegs Made by Ian Harwood and John Isaacs, England

spinets, viols and lutes. Dolmetsch remained in the States running this department until 1910. His department for Paris resulted in a period of non-activity in harpsichord building that lasted until 1931, when John Challis, who had trained with Dolmetsch, re-introduced this craft to the States. It is interesting to consider that during the second world war Challis' workshop must have been one of the very few where harpsichord production continued. William Dowd in turn received his training at the John Challis atelier and in 1949 the Hubbard and Dowd partnership was formed

in Boston. The work done by these two men could be said to have had a revolutionary influence on harpsichord building in the world. Their main concern was a return to 17th and 18th century traditions and principles of construction. One of their harpsichords, based upon a French instrument made by Pascal Taskin (1723–1793), was bought by the Paris-based harpsichordist Kenneth Gilbert and brought to Britain in 1967, where it had a considerable influence on the methods of building in British workshops.

186, 187 Baroque Guitar; based on an instrument made by Giorgio Jungman in 1633, held in the collection of the Conservatoire Royal de Musique at Brussels; maple, spruce, ebony, pearwood

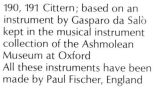

188, 189 Vihuela de Mano; originally the Spanish word 'vihuela' applied to any type of stringed instrument. In the Renaissance it came to have a limited application to a plucked instrument similar to a guitar of the time but having six, rather than four courses of strings; cypress, spruce, ebony, ivory, gut and parchment

190, 191 Cittern; based on an instrument by Gasparo da Salò kept in the musical instrument collection of the Ashmolean Museum at Oxford
All these instruments have been made by Paul Fischer, England

After working in Paris for Gaveau's, a French piano manufacturer, Arnold Dolmetsch established a workshop in Haslemere in Surrey, England, in 1918 and in 1925 began a series of music festivals which have continued to the present day. In his Haslemere workshop Dolmetsch concentrated on the production of a wide range of musical instruments. Whereas his work in America had resulted essentially in the revitalization of the harpsichord, the Haslemere workshop now became the source from which the revival of other instruments grew, most notably the woodwind family.

192, 193, 194 Viol; this particular
maker bases all his instruments
on viols made between 1660 and
1730. In each instance he has
studied the original instrument
minutely, sometimes restoring it
and taking measurements which,
after allowing for the age
of the timber, he reproduces
within one tenth of a millimetre
Made by Michael Goater, England

PLUS FAIT DOUCEUR QUE VIOLENCE

195 Unfretted Clavichord, 1977; the popularity of the clavichord, a forerunner of the pianoforte, spans from the 14th to the 18th century. This four-octave example is freely based on a 16th century Italian prototype illustrated in Michael Praetorius's treaty. Its maker produced every part of it: case and stand, of one piece of English lime, lacquered; brass strap hinges, handpierced and engraved; strings of steel covered with laminated gold; key covers of Indian ebony and elephant ivory. The instrument could be played resting on a table; 1 × 33·6m (39·5" × 13¼") height with stand 75 (29½")
Made by Alan Grove, England

photography : Alan Curtis

Today the name Dolmetsch is synonimous with the recorder.

Inevitably, acknowledgement for the serious growth of interest in the performance of early music on wind instruments is due to those performers who have brought it to the attention of the public: Frans Brueggen, on the recorder, and David Munrow on a variety of

196 Baryton; a brass stringed instrument evolved in the late 17th century, the baryton is similar in tone quality and range to the bass viol. Haydn wrote 175 works for this instrument for his patron Prince Nicholas Esterhazy
Made by Michael Heale, England

197, 198 Two views of a Baroque violin
Made by Jaap Bolink, Holland

199 Harpsichord; modelled on an instrument by Andreas Ruckers made in 1638, the materials and methods of construction reproduce as far as possible those of the Flemish original
Made by Adlam & Burnett, England

wind instruments.

Brueggen, who at the age of 21 was appointed professor of recorder at the Royal Highschool of Music at the Hague and at the Amsterdam Conservatoire, has taught students from the United States, Japan, Germany, Sweden, Austria and Switzerland as well as those from his native country, Holland. He has catalogued all the finest specimens of 18th century recorders in existence and recorded their sound in a three-record album. Undoubtedly the availability of such recordings has accelerated the international response to the performance of early music and the consequent demand has led to the reconstruction of instruments, for not everyone is fortunate enough to possess original instruments.

David Munrow, published a set of recordings and a book describing all the instruments of the Middle Ages and the Renaissance shortly before his death, in 1976. In these recordings he performs brilliantly on medieval and Renaissance shawms, reed pipes, bagpipes, bladder pipes, flutes and recorders. Until his tragically early death he was, along with Frans Brueggen, the most outstanding international woodwind performer. His radio and concert performances were responsible for familiarizing vast audiences with hitherto unfamiliar music and the key to his success was that he was able to combine scholarship with a lively and catalystic enthusiasm.

The 1960s saw the emergence of several early music groups which have had a profound influence on the musical taste of audiences the world over. Musica Reservata, founded by John Beckett and Michael Morrow was one such, and David Munrow's Early Music Consort, the Vienna Concentus Musicus formed by Nicholas Harnoncourt, and the Leonhardt Consort formed by Gustav Leonhardt in Holland, all became renowned for the quality of their recordings of early music performed on 'original' instruments. By the 1970s more and more early music consorts were formed. In London alone, groups such as Antony Rooley's Consort of Musicke and the English Concert directed by Trevor Pinnock had been added to the growing list of reputable groups concentrating on the performance of early music.

In 1973 a quarterly publication entitled 'Early Music' was launched by Oxford University Press under the editorship of John Thomson, and in the few ensuing years the magazine has grown and extended its range to include reviews and articles about performances, conferences and festivals all over the world. Colleges such as the London College of Furniture have begun to include courses on musical instrument technology in their programmes, and more frequent exhibitions of musical instruments are becoming a part of the year's musical calendar.

In Holland a revival of interest in the harpsichord occurred in the 1950s. This was very largely due to the work of Gustav Leonhardt and as a result of the increased interest in the performances of early music, which he generated, builders of instruments began to emerge. Between 1900 and the 1950s there had been no instrument building in Holland. Factory production of harpsichords, general in France, Germany and England, was not found in Holland and it was only in the 1960s that builders such as Gerrit Klop, W. Jiskoot and Farma en Raetgever began to construct harpsichords and spinets based upon the 17th and 18th century traditions. They were followed in the 1970s by the van Emmerick brothers of Utrecht and by J Klinkhamer and W Kroesbergen of Utrecht. Many of the instruments produced in Holland are based upon those built by the house of Ruckers, the great harpsichord building family living in the

200 Decorative rose of a muselar, modelled on an instrument made by Andreas Ruckers in 1611
Made by Adlam & Burnett, England

Opposite
201 Full view of the soundboard of a double manual cembalo, based on a 1769 original by Pascal Taskin. Note how the painting reflects the style of the period
Made by Eckehart Merzdorf, West Germany

Netherlands in the 16th century. This holds good for some of the finest instruments being constructed in Britain too, by makers of the highest reputation such as Derek Adlam, of the Adlam–Burnett partnership, and David Rubio. Most of these makers are perpetually beset with appeals to turn more and more of their time to the work of reconstruction and the preservation of the instruments in the great collections of the world.

Without the cooperation of the great Museums the work of reconstruction would, of necessity, be a great deal more difficult. Credit, no doubt, should be given to those amazing figures of the 16th and 17th centuries who amassed collections of instruments; François 1er of France, Henry VIII of England, Isabella d'Este, the Marchioness of Mantua, the Duke of Ferrara and the Archduke Ferdinand of Tyrol. Parts of their collections have come down to us and are today in different parts of the world, made available for measurement and study by sympathetic museum curators.

In the United States of America the Crosby-Brown Collection of Musical Instruments of All Nations, in the Metropolitan Museum in New York, is the earliest and also the largest collection of musical instruments in the Northern Hemisphere. Begun in the 1870s, in Florence, with the purchase of an ivory lute by Mrs John Crosby-Brown, it now includes instruments from Europe, Asia, Africa, America and Oceania and contains approximately 4,000 instruments.

In Britain the Victoria and Albert Museum, the Horniman Museum, and the Benton-Fletcher collection of working keyboard instruments, in Fenton House, the Russell Collection in Edinburgh and the Ashmolean Museum in Oxford offer the student opportunity for study and reconstruction.

Norway has the Ringve Museum in Trondheim, with about 600 instruments from all over the world, acquired originally between 1946 and 1963 by Victoria and Christian Auher Bachke, who established and endowed the Museum. Even contemporary makers such as Peter Harlan, who makes recorders and viols, are represented.

In Germany the Germanisches National Museum in Nuremberg contains, in addition to German instruments, Italian and Flemish keyboard instruments, a French harpsichord from about 1700, a flute made by Charles Bizey of Paris in 1736 and various others from Britain, France and Italy. Many were destroyed in 1945 but since the 1960s the collection has grown to the size of 2,000 instruments, collected by Dr Ulrich Ruck and includes part of the Neupert Collection.

Holland is fortunate in the existence of the Gemeentie Museum at the Hague, and the Bussum Museum near Amsterdam which contains the Carol van Leeuwen Boomkamp collection.

In France the most important collection is to be found in Paris, at the Musée Instrumental of the Paris Conservatoire. The guiding spirit behind this collection was the remarkable Geneviève Thibault, who died in August 1975 while working on her extremely successful travelling exhibition 'Eighteenth Century Musical Instruments: France and Britain'. She had been working on a Directory of the World's Musical Instrument Collections up until the moment of her death.

In Vienna the Kunsthistorisches Museum contains the famous Ambras Collection. In Italy there are collections in Bologna, at the Museo Civico, in Florence, in Milan, and at the Museo degli Strumenti Musicali in Rome. Venice has lost the greater part of the Correr Collection to Brussels. As to Belgium, the Vleeshuis in Antwerp is of great interest and Brussels has some of the collection of A Tolbecque of Paris. Most of the Correr Collection from Venice is in the Conservatoire Royal de Musique. There are probably many omissions in such a list, but certainly a would-be maker would find that a tour of these museums would furnish him with ample material for study.

The climate then, in 1978, is a productive one. Instrument makers are finding that more assistance is forthcoming from government bodies for research and workshop grants. Curators of Museums are cooperative and the public has an unassuaged appetite for the type of music performed on early instruments. The anachronism remains while John Cage, who once spent two years working in the computer studios of Illinois University to produce a work called HPSCHD, exists beside the individuals who perform the music of Lorenzo de' Medici's era on instruments as nearly as possible approximating those of his time. The possibilities for musical composition and performance can scarcely ever have been so wide.

Trends in Furnishing and Decorative Art

202 'Spatial Ikat', 1977; hand woven ikat tapestry; wool and jute weft, warp of expanded polyurethane of varying thickness 3·15 × 2·75m (10′ 6″ × 9′ 0″) Made by Lia Cook, USA

Below
203 Head with relief figures, 1976; cast bone china, hand polished; 17 (7″) high Made by Glenys Barton for Wedgwood, England

204 Enamelled panel, 1977; jewelry enamel and diluted gum tragacanth are applied to specially prepared low carbon steel and allowed to dry before the basic grid is scratched through and panel fired at 800°C; subsequent coats are then applied using various techniques such as wet spraying and dry stencilling; 25 × 25 (10″ × 10″) Made by Amal Ghosh, England

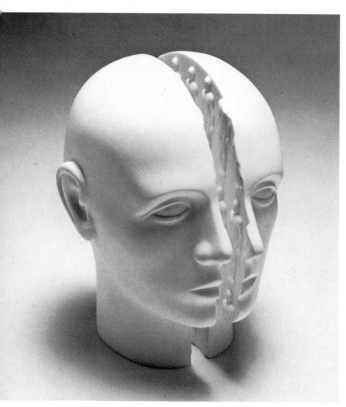

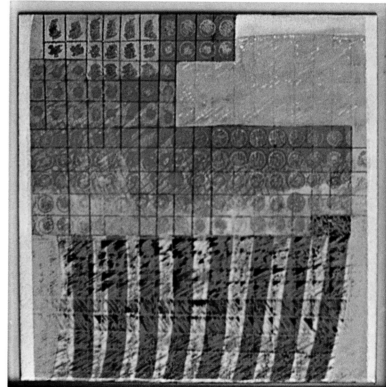

205 'Foxtrot'; pendant lamp; steel wires tipped with rubber grip the glass globe in position; polished steel and blown glass Ø 60 (2′ 0″)
Designed by Ennio Chiggio for Lumenform, Italy

206 Lounging chair and foot-stool, from a range that also includes dining chairs and settee; natural ash and French cane
Designed by Rud Thygesen and Johnny Sørensen for Christensen and Larsen, Denmark

207, 208 Armchair and sofa from
the DS-47 range; the seat slides
forward for a more relaxed
position; upholstered in thick
hide
Made by De Sede, West
Germany

209 'Cobra', table lamp;
articulated rubber body,
black casing of synthetic
material
Designed by Masayuki Kurokawa
for Yamagiwa Lamp, Japan

210 Pocket lighter, table
lighter and ashtray prototypes;
case of metal with polished brass
decoration on black body
Designed by Carla Venosta and
Guido Zimmermann for
Oggett s.r.l. Italy

211 Bowl; hand blown, clear or
grey Murano crystal glass; 13,
18·5 or 25 (5″, 7¼″ or 9¾″) high
Designed by Flavio Barbini for
Barbini Vetreria, Italy

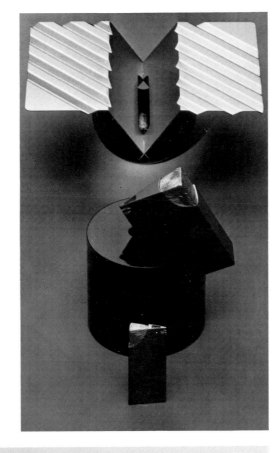

212 'Reticolo', occasional table;
a single sheet of 7mm (¼″) wired
glass is heated, then bent on a
former 1·20m × 80 × 35 (3′11″ ×
2′8″ × 1′2″)
Designed by Angelo Cortesi for
FIAM, Italy

150

Left
213 'after "Black Disk on Tan" by Adolph Gottlieb'; one of a limited edition of five tapestries; wool and linen weft on cotton warp, 2·10 × 1·70m (7'0" × 5'6") Produced and edited by Gloria F Ross Tapestries, New York Made at the Dovecot Studio, Scotland

214 Earthenware pot with fire marks, unglazed
Made by Roberta Marks, USA

215, 216 'Jeans', stackable chair; natural or dark brown canvas on steel frame; chrome or plastified yellow finish Designed and made by A & L Verhaegen S.A., Belgium

217 'Ezile', wine carafe; glass
and silver plated metal
Designed by Lino Sabattini for
Argenteria Sabattini, Italy

Below
218 Three-legged table, 1976;
the stand is in the shape of a
double tripod, one inverted;
solid bird's eye maple with
tulip wood inlays
Designed and made by
Rupert Williamson, England

219 Blanket chest; figured
English oak; 51 × 51 × 1·02m
(20″ × 20″ × 40″)
Designed and made by Peter
Milne at the Ravensbourne
College of Art and Design,
England

220, 221 'Wireless Lamps', 1976;
prototypes of fluorescent cord-
less lamps operated within a
given range by a micro-wave
transmitter (not shown);
acrylic rods 2·5 × 2·5 × 14, 22
or 30 (1″ × 1″ × 5½″, 8¾″ or
11¾″); glass sphere 9 (3½″) ∅
Designed by Shoei Yoh for
Matsuya Plastics and
Yamagiwa Glass, Japan

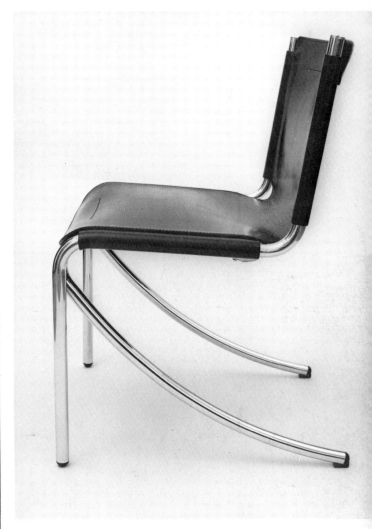

222 'Jot', demountable chair;
saddle leather body on polished
chrome frame, with optional arm
rests (not shown); black, red,
maroon or natural; 60 × 50 × 80
(2′ 0″ × 1′ 8″ × 2′ 8″)
Designed by Giotto Stoppino for
Acerbis International, Italy

153

223 'Mali', chair; laminated
poplarwood, 1·10m × 51 × 95
(3′ 7″ × 1′ 8″ × 3′ 1″)
Designed by Raffaella Vallecchi
for G. Pedano SaS, Italy

224 'Reflets blancs II', 1977;
environmental tapestry, haute
lisse technique; wool, silk and
goat hair; 3m × 5m × 1·50m
(9′ 11″ × 6′ 5″ × 4′ 11″)
Made by Jagoda Buíc,
Yugoslavia

225 'Elogio' suite; units convert
to single or double beds; dacron
and expanded polyurethane on
steel frame; corner unit 1·40m
(4′7″), centre unit 1·02m (3′11″)
long; 1·06m (3′6″) deep
Designed by Afra and Tobia
Scarpa for B & B Spa, Italy

Below
226 'Albadine', chair;
upholstered seat, varnished bent
ash frame
Designed by Franco Bazzani for
Alberto Bazzani, Italy

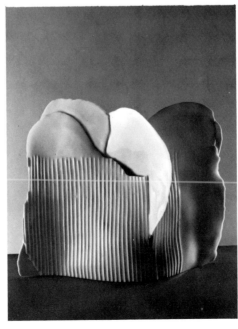

227 'Folded form with fan';
slab built white porcelain
40 × 34 (16″ × 13″)
Made by Kurt and Gerda Spurey,
Austria

228 'after "Flin Flon XIII" by
Frank Stella'; one of an edition
of seven tapestries; wool weft
on cotton warp; 2·68 × 2·68m
(8′ 10″ × 8′ 10″)
Produced and edited by Gloria F
Ross, New York
Made at the Pinton Atelier

229 'Ferrara', range of drinking
glasses; mouth blown
Designed by Piero D'Alfonso for
Peruzzi & Bozzi, Italy

230 'Chinese Ivory', stainless
steel, dish-washer proof
cutlery
Designed by David Mellor for
David Mellor Cutlery, England

231, 232, 233 Trestle table and
folding chair; cane seat, laminated bent ash frame, natural
finish; 1·40m × 75 × 72 (55" ×
$29\frac{1}{2}'' × 28\frac{1}{4}''$)
Designed by Giovanni Offredi
for Crassevig, Italy

234 'Maggia', range of chairs
and settees convertible into
single or double beds by
sliding open the interlocking
elements of the base; bent ash,
97 × 75 (3′ 2″ × 2′ 6″); 80, 1·20m,
1·60m (2′ 7″, 3′ 11″, 5′ 3″) long
Designed by De Pas, D'Urbino &
Lomazzi for multi-Gufram, Italy

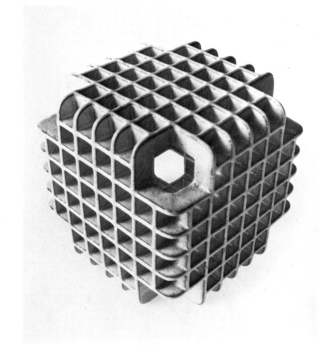

235 Sculptural Object; extruded
majolica with dolomite glaze;
about 40 (1′ 4″)
Designed and made by
Alessio Tasca, Italy

236 'Triedro', swivelling lamp;
shown here with a clip mounting,
the lamp can also be used with
a lighting track; white enamel
metal with black holder, silvered
bulb
Designed by Joe Colombo for
Stilnovo, Italy

237, 238, 239 'Eletto', convertible
sofa, opens to reveal the bed
already made up; separate
storage for pillows; upholstered
with leather
Designed by Paolo Piva for
B & B, Italy

240 'Jyta', children's modular
furniture for self assembly;
units can be joined together
by metal pins to form tables
settees, cots, beds and shelving;
chipboard, lacquered red or
white
Designed by Jaakko Halko for
Lepokalusto Oy, Finland

241 Furnishing fabric; screen-
print on 85% cotton 15% rayon
mixture, 140 (4′8″) wide
Designed by Paiu Konttinen for
Oy Finlayson Ab Porin Puuvilla,
Finland

Opposite
242, 243 Toys of solid wood,
oiled and polished; hand formed
metal connectors; train 1·20m
long, 14 wide, 29 high (47″ ×
$5\frac{1}{2}$″ × $9\frac{3}{4}$″); truck 10·5 × 16·5 × 25
(16″ × $6\frac{1}{2}$″ × $9\frac{3}{4}$″)
Made by Michael Parker for
Columbia River Toy Works, USA

244 'Fabel' child's chair, with
playing/eating tray and seat
adjustable to eight heights;
laid on its side the chair
becomes a play horse or a
bench for two; two units linked
together form a cradle; natural,
red or green stained beech,
43 × 54 × 67·5 (2′ 3″ × 1′ 9″ ×
2′ $2\frac{3}{4}$″)
Designed by J. Daãe-Quale
for Westnofa, Norway

245, 246, 247, 248, 249 '3000',
range of bathroom furniture;
units come in multiples of 30, 60
(1' 0'', 2' 0'') and are fitted with
specially designed accessories of
moulded polystyrene; illustrated
here are details of shelf with
swivel storage trays; corner unit;
mirror cabinet and laundry
container units; yellow, with
white or wood-grain doors
Designed by Dr. Schürer for
Poggenpohl, West Germany

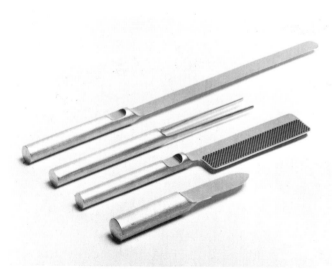

Left

250 'Polidada', integral kitchen system; structure of upright and horizontal panels. A series of holes placed at 32mm intervals along the lateral uprights allows a flexible vertical adjustment of horizontal planes; service units include a range of coordinated appliances such as sinks, stoves, dishwashers and refrigerators; 30, 45, 60, 90 (1' 0", 1' 6", 2' 0", 3' 0") wide; 39·4, 58·6 (1' 3", 1' 11") deep; 85, 2·17, 2·69m (2' 7", 7' 1", 8' 10") high
Designed by George Coslin for A Garavaglia Sas, Italy

251 Carving set and two cheese knives from a range of table accessories
Designed by OPI Milano for Cini & Nils, Italy

252 Place setting for airline passengers; melamine tray, china, glass, stainless steel
Designed by Joe Colombo and Ambrogio Pozzi for Alitalia, Italy

Above

253 Range of demountable dining furniture of various sizes, comprising tables, chairs and cabinets. A choice of finishes includes solid wood or linoleum-covered table tops; cord or webbing woven seats, with optional armrests for the chairs; painted doors. The whole range may be easily assembled without the aid of tools; beech, oak or mahogany
Designed by Dr. Bernt for Kventy & Sønner, Denmark

254 Bar set; stainless steel with satin finish
Designed by Salvatore Gregorietti for Coppola & Parodi, Italy

255 Chair, 1975; note the twin u-frame supporting the body; laminated beech, woven jute bands
Designed by Rud Thygesen and Johnny Sørensen for Magnus Olesen, Denmark

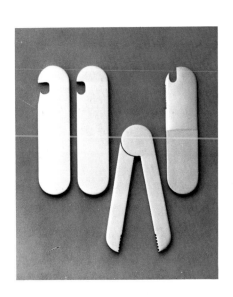

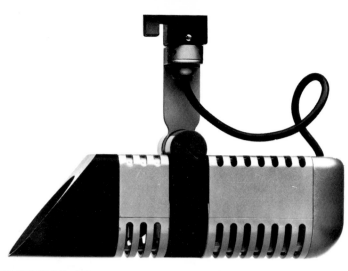

256 'Pinspot', from a range of
display light fittings; low
voltage, fully adjustable spot-
lamp available with bracket or
for use with a lighting track;
die cast synthetic material,
silver with black and red
trimmings
Designed by Roger Tallon for
ERCO, West Germany

257 'Talking Office', open plan
modular furniture; work tops
and storage units are fixed to die
cast aluminium frames; baize
covered screen on steel frames
can support vertical files; work
tops are faced with laminate,
1·30, 1·50, 1·80m (3' 11", 4' 11",
5' 11") long, 75 (2' 6") deep;
screens 75, 1·20, 1·50m (2' 6",
3' 11", 4' 11") long
Designed by Alberto Rosselli
for Facomet, Italy

258, 259 'Baltic', open plan
office system; desks, cabinets
and storage units with suspended
filing (see detail); chipboard,
with crown oak veneer
Designed and made by Dodson
Bull, England

Opposite
260 'Dialogo' chair; natural ash
or leather covered body, fixed
to ash bearers or to chrome
finish steel frame
Designed by Afra and Tobia
Scarpa for B & B, Italy

261 Cigarette container and ashtray from the 'Erica' range, 1975; engraved amethyst crystal with silver lid
Designed by Sergio Asti for Cristalleria Imperatore, Italy

Below
262 'Extended Cube', miniature textile sculpture in nylon monofilament; 15 (6") approximately
Made by Ann Sutton, England

263 Glass dish, 1976; free blowing technique, with undercasing decoration of coloured glass pieces; 32 (1'1") wide
Made by Dillon Clarke, England

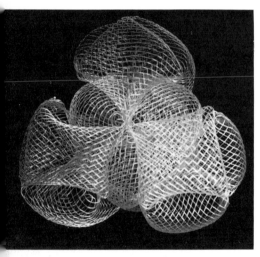

Opposite
264, 265 Jewelry case; steam bent kingwood, with dovetailing pins of holly; maroon velvet lining
Designed and made by S P Hounslow at the Royal College of Art, England

266 'Laminex', demountable chair in two interlocking pieces; 18mm laminated beech, natural finish or rosewood veneer; 54 × 74 × 70 (1'9" × 2'5" × 2'4")
Designed by Jens Nielsen for Falster Form a/s, Denmark

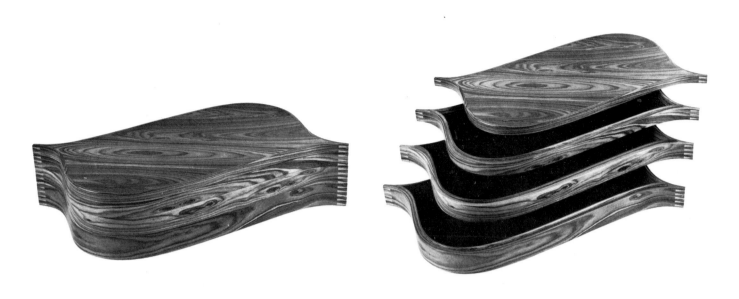

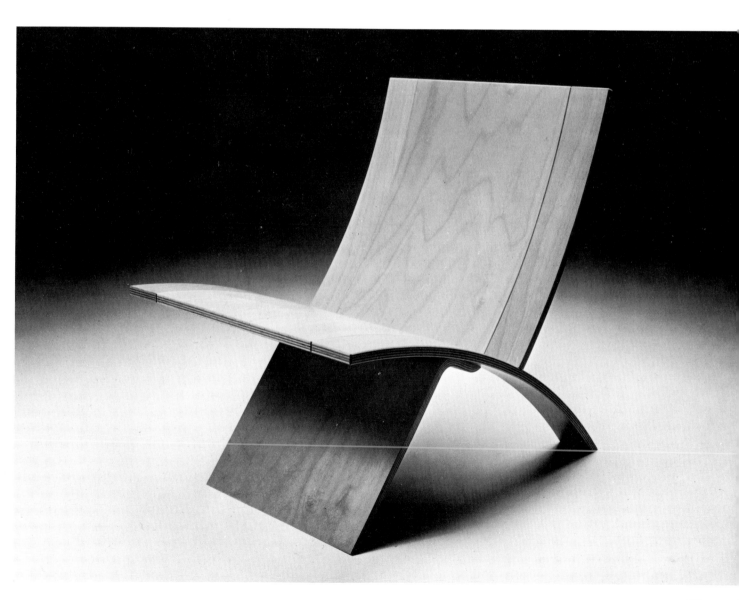

267 Bracelet with four garnets;
14 carat gold
Made by Thor Selzer, Denmark

268 Brooch, 1976; 18 carat gold
with precious and semi-precious
stones
Made by Wendy Ramshaw,
England

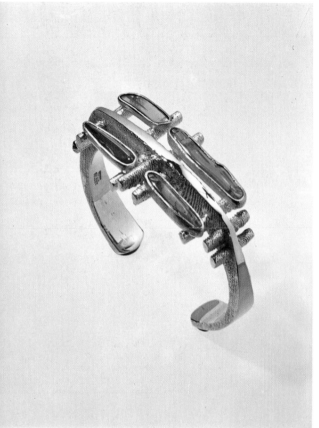

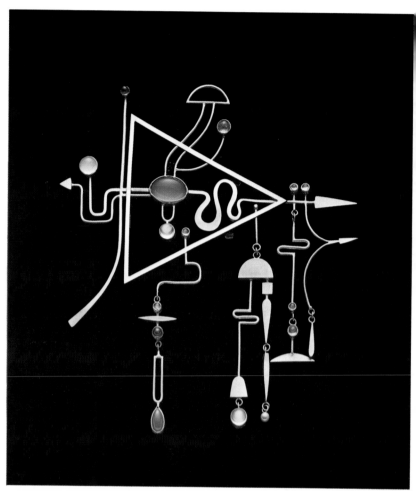

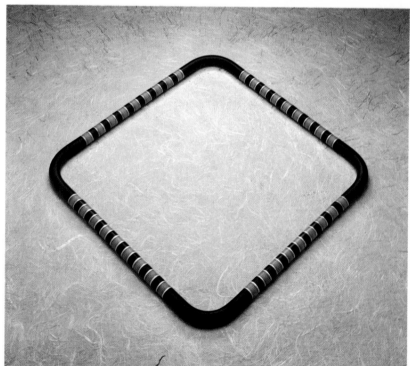

269 Neckpiece, 1976; acrylic,
with 18 carat gold inlays
Made by David Watkins, England

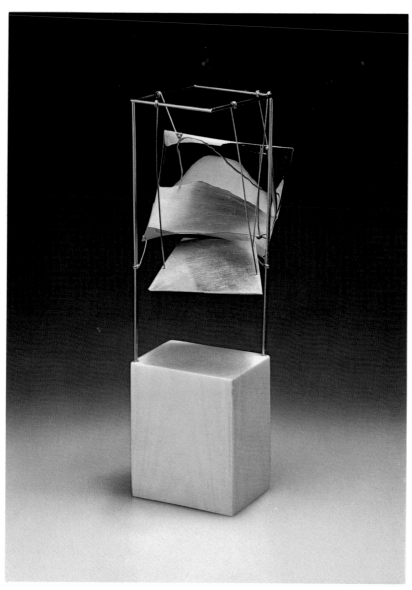

270 'Stage', 1977; 14 and 18 carat gold on ivory base; 20 × 7 (8″ × 3″)
Made by Ole Bent Petersen, Denmark

271, 272 'Major Egmont Brodie-Williams in Africa', 1977; series of engravings on crystal goblets, unique pieces; the detail is from 'The Major and the Turtles'; 15 (6″) high
Engraved by Ronald Pennell, England

273 Stoneware pot; hand thrown, with wax resist ash glaze and combed decoration; 46 (18″) high
Made by William Wilhelmi, USA

Below
274 SL 544/25 teapot, 1976; hand made; sterling silver with rosewood handle
Made by Sigurd Persson, Sweden

275 'Corolle', range of crystal wine glasses, mould-blown; 23, 28, 33 (9″, 11″, 13″) high
Designed and made by Daum, Cristallerie de Nancy, France

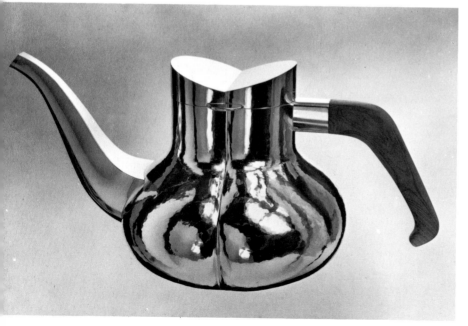

Left
276 'Onda', pendant lamp;
mouth blown Murano crystal
glass; 35 × 45 Ø (1′ 2″ × 1′ 6″ Ø)
Designed by Renato Toso
for Leucos srl, Italy

277 This silver chest – potentially
an uninteresting form – pleases
by the understated elegance of
its stand, the invitation of the
pulls (finished by knife), the
logicality of the connecting
knuckles which are the fulcrum
of the piece. A drawer may be
put on top: grooves receive it
and the surface is unharmed;
oiled Swedish maple, 47 × 38 × 74
(1′ 6″ × 1′ 3″ × 2′ 5″)
Made by James Krenov, Sweden

The cabinets on the following
pages, both made in 1977, may
be considered as concave and
convex variations on a theme.
James Krenov designs always
repay careful studies. This
craftsman seeks simplicity,
avoiding any showy effect; his
aim is to let the beauty of the
wood speak for itself and the
appeal of the work derives from
the subtle relationships gradually
establishing themselves. Note in
the elm cabinet the compound
curve and shaping of the sides,
the gouge marks on the top and
its lower height: in the pearwood
piece the concavity is carried
gently throughout from the
doors, the drawers and shelf, to
the stretchers joining the
tapered legs – closer at the front
than the back

photography:
Bengt Carlén

278, 279, 280 Cabinet, 1977;
pearwood body; drawers of
Lebanon cedar with fronts of
rosewood; stand of Spanish
veroola; 1·58 × 45 × 18 (4′11″ ×
1′6″ × 7″)

174

281, 282, 283 Cabinet 1977;
entirely made of solid elm,
natural finish 1·35 × 53 × 25
(4'5" × 1'9" × 10")
All designed and made by
James Krenov, Sweden

284 Container, 1975; four pink
cubes within a blue frame on a
green base; the design
emphasizes the contrast
between volume and structure;
lacquered wood

285 Container, 1974; green and
yellow volume within a white
frame; structure and volume
appear independent of each
other, an impression emphasized
by a mirror at the base
of the frame; lacquered wood

286 Container, 1974; this piece
was influenced by Egyptian
originals, the design for the
handles being taken from a
chest belonging to
Tutankhamun; white lacquered
wood

Opposite
287 Double seat in the style of
a throne, 1974; the back and
base appear to be divided, but
are in fact one piece, an effect
increased by the colour contrast;
lacquered wood
All designed by Pieter de Bruyne
Belgium

288 'WXYZ' 1976; range of non-functional chairs; 15mm plate glass glued with 'Photobond 100', a product giving a glass to glass sheer adhesion of 33·4 Kg/cm²; 'Photobond 100' cures by the action of ultra-violet rays, therefore at least one of the surfaces to be glued must be transparent
Designed by Shoei Yoh for Kihami Glass Works, Japan

289 Stoneware pot, 1977; slab built with sprayed and inlaid decoration; 24 (9½″) high
Made by Jacqui Poncelet, England

290 Ceramic objects; hand pressed and fired at a low temperature; 9 (3½) wide
Made by Candido Fior, Italy

291 Silver necklace; hand beaten concave links joined by heavy rings
Made by Avreli Bisbe, Spain

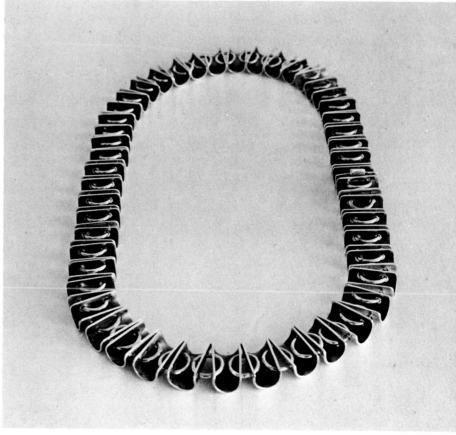

292, 293 Two stoneware panels;
each 1·60 × 2m (4' 11" × 6' 6")
approximately
Designed by Juan Vilagrau and
made by Jordy Aguade for
La Cantonada, Spain

Manufacturers and Designers

Acerbis International
via Brusaporto 31
Seriate (Bergamo)
Italy

Derek Adlam & Richard Burnett
Finchcocks
Goudhurst
Kent
England

Jordi Aguade & Juan Vila Grau
c/o La Cantonada
Freixa 2
Barcelona
Spain

Christopher Allworth
RR3-1110 Yarmouth
Nova Scotia B5A 4A7
Canada

B & B Italia Spa
strada Provinciale
22060 Novedrate (Como)
Italy

Barbini Vetreria
Fondamenta Venier 48
30121 Murano (Venezia)
Italy

Glenys Barton
c/o CAC
12 Waterloo Place
London SW1
England

Alberto Bazzani
via Pusteria 37
20030 Bovisio (Milano)
Italy

Avreli Bisbe
Provenca 261
Edifiçi La Pedrera
Barcelona
Spain

Jaap Bolink
Jan van Eijckstraat 24
Amsterdam
Holland

Pieter de Bruyne
Stationsstraat 15
Aalst
Belgium

Jagoda Buić
c/o Marković
11000 Beograd
3 Dositejeva
Yugoslavia

Cini & Nils Sas
via F Ferruccio 8
20145 Milano
Italy

Columbia River Toy Works
2824 NW Santanita Terrace
Portland, Or 97210
USA

Lia Cook
1438 Grove Street
Berkeley, Cal 94709
USA

Coppola & Parodi
via Marco d'Agrate 41
Milano
Italy

John Cousen
Thornley House
393 Bradford Road
Fartown
Huddersfield
Yorkshire
England

Crassevig
via Trieste 24
33040 Corno di Rosazzo (Udine)
Italy

Daum Cristallerie de Nancy
32 rue de Paradis
Paris 10
France

De Sede AG
Ch-5313 Klingnau
Switzerland

Dodson Bull Interiors
Barbican Trade Centre
Barbican
London EC2
England

Arnold Dolmetsch Ltd.
Kings Road
Haslemere
Surrey
England

ERCO Leuchten GmbH
Postfach 2460
5880 Lüdenscheid
West Germany

Facomet
via Ripamonti 89
20139 Milano
Italy

Falster Form A/S
Gedsvej 38
DK-4800 Nykøbing F
Denmark

FIAM
c/o Carla Caccia
via Bramante 32
Milano
Italy

Candido Fior
c/o Carla Caccia
via Bramante 32
Milano
Italy

Paul Fischer
Rubio Workshop
The Ridge House
Duns Tew
Oxford
England

Lynn Fisher
The Pottery
1 The Grove
London N4
England

Peter Forrester
Sunflower House
Beechwood Avenue
Aylmerton
Norfolk
England

A Garavaglia Sas
strada Provinciale 31
20010 Mesero (Milano)
Italy

Amal Ghosh
9 Lilyville Road
London SW6

Michael Goater
Moor House
Butleigh
nr Glastonbury
Somerset
England

Alan Grove
5 Land Oak Drive
Kidderminster
Worcestershire
England

John Hanchet
57 Ward Avenue
Grays
Essex
England

Ian Harwood & John Isaacs
18 Barton Road
Ely
Cambridge
England

Michael Heale
14 Market Street
Guildford
Surrey
England

James Krenov
43 Anundsvägen
16154 Bromma
Sweden

Kventy & Sønner Stolefabrik A/S
Toftebakken 4–8
DK-3460 Birkerød
Denmark

Lepokalusto Oy
15540 Villähde
Finland

Leucos Snc
via Treviso 65
30037 Scorze (Venezia)
Italy

Lumenform
via Rinascita 95/a
30175 Marghera (Venezia)
Italy

Matsuya Plastics
c/o Matsuya Department Store
3-6-1 Ginza
Chuo-ku
Tokyo
Japan

David Mellor
4 Sloane Square
London SW1
England

Eckehart Merzdorf
D-7537 Remchingen
Ortsteil Wilferdingen
Bahnhofstraße 6
West Germany

Peter Milne
23 Mossford Street
Mile End
London E3
England

Christopher Monk
Stock Farm House
Churt
Farnham
Surrey
England

multi-Gufram Snc
via Taneschie 14
10073 Ciriè (Torino)
Italy

John Nicholson
Breame House
Hungershall Park
Tunbridge Wells
Kent
England

Oggett srl
c/o Studio Venosta
via Lovanio 6
Milan
Italy

Magnus Olesen A/S
Tønderingvej
Durup
DK-7870 Roslev
Denmark

Pedano Sas
viale Umbria 126
20135 Milano
Italy

Ronald Pennell
2 Lower Bibbletts
Hoarwithy
Hereford
England

Sigurd Persson
Höbergsgatan
11645 Stockholm
Sweden

Peruzzi & Bozzi
c/o Carla Caccia
via Bramante 32
Milano
Italy

Ole Bent Petersen
Poul Ankersgade 2
Copenhagen
DK-1271
Denmark

Poggenpohl AG
49 Herford
Bünderstrasse 103
West Germany

Jacqui Poncelet
c/o CAC
Waterloo Place
London SW1
England

Porin Puuvilla Oy
Pori
Finland

Wendy Ramshaw
c/o CAC
12 Waterloo Place
London SW1
England

Sam Rizzetta
Rt 1 Box 362A
Barboursville, Va 22923
USA

Gloria F Ross
21 East 87 Street (Apt 6c)
New York NY 10028
USA

Sabattini Argenteria
via A Volta
22072 Bregnano (Como)
Italy

Thor Selzer
Skindergade 44
Copenhagen K
DK-1159
Denmark

Kurt and Gerda Spurey
Schuttelstraße 49
1020 Vienna
Austria

Stilnovo Spa
via F Ferruccio 8
20145 Milano
Italy

Ann Sutton
Parnham House
Beaminster
Dorset
England

Alessio Tasca Ceramiche
via Roberti 15
36055 Nove (Vicenza)
Italy

David Watkins,
c/o CAC
12 Waterloo Place
London SW1
England

Westnofa A/S
PO Box 83
6151 Ørsta
Norway

William Wilhelmi
1129 Ocean Drive
Corpus Christi, Tx 78404
USA

R. Williamson
5 Goddard Croft
Greenleys
Milton Keynes
England

Denzil Wraight
1 Ashton Street
Oxford
England

Yamagiwa Lamp
c/o Masayuki Kurokawa
Flat Aoyama 101
5-15-9 Minami-Aoyama
Minato-ku
Tokyo
Japan